Inside

Essays on Hold 'em and General Poker Concepts

By
John Feeney Ph.D.

A product of Two Plus Two Publishing

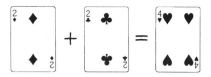

FIRST EDITION

THIRD PRINTING
February 2003

Printing and Binding
Creel Printing Co.
Las Vegas, Nevada

Printed in the United States of America

For information contact: **Two Plus Two Publishing**
                             226 Garfield Dr.
                             Henderson NV 89014
                             (702) 896-1326

ISBN: 1-880685-26-4

Table of Contents

Foreword
by Mason Malmuth

To become an expert poker player you need to master two general areas that deal with your strategic play. First, you need to learn and understand the many skills that the game requires. This includes concepts such as hand selection, position, knocking other players out, bluffing, semi-bluffing, deception, proper image projection, and reading hands. The second area is simply putting all these ideas and concepts together in a manner that can devastate and totally confuse your weaker opponents while allowing you to hold your own against other expert players.

Accomplishing all of this is not easy. Over the years I have had conversations with many players who had become quite adept in the first area. That is they knew and understood all the appropriate skills and could "talk" quite a good game. A couple of these people have even made reputations for themselves by winning a tournament or two. But "when the dust settled" so to speak, they were all at best only small winners. And when they stepped up in limit and challenged the better players, they almost always failed. You see, knowing the concepts is one thing, putting it all together is another.

This text, written by John Feeney, is about putting it all together. Besides having a Ph.D. in psychology, John has become an expert poker player who has graduated to and achieved success at the upper middle limits and higher. There are only a handful of players who can legitimately make this claim.

The success that John achieved did not come overnight. It took a lot of thinking as well as a thorough and systematic approach to the game.

When we at Two Plus Two Publishing LLC first saw this material, we couldn't believe how good it was. From "Playing Too Many Hands," to "Self-Weighting Cold Calls," to "Short-Handed Play: Don't Miss Out," to "The Strategic Moment in Hold 'em," to "Countering a Good Reader," to "A Poker Player in Therapy," to "Thoughts on the Effects of the Poker Literature,"... John shows us *exactly* how to put it all together and take those concepts which some of you have struggled with for so long, and convert them into true winning play.

In closing, let me say that this will be one of the most important poker books that you will ever read. Assuming you are willing to do your homework, and study what Dr. Feeney talks about in this text. *Inside the Poker Mind: Essays on Hold 'em and General Poker Concepts* along with the proper how to and poker theory books, can make a big difference in your game.

About John Feeney

John Feeney spent his youth in Phoenix Arizona. After attending the University of Colorado he moved to San Diego to pursue graduate work in clinical psychology at the California School of Professional Psychology. His interest in poker was sparked while observing a hold 'em game during a weekend trip to Las Vegas. True to his background, he took an academic approach to the game, studying the poker literature, consulting with David Sklansky, and getting the requisite playing experience. By the time he received his Ph.D., poker was beginning to compete with psychology for his attention. He soon began to log more hours in the cardrooms of Southern California than in his field of psychology, until ultimately poker became his primary focus.

Today John can often be found in mid-limit and higher games in San Diego, Los Angeles, or elsewhere. When not at the tables John now devotes a good portion of his time to writing. His articles in *Poker Digest* have been well received, and he is a regular participant in poker discussions on the Internet. You can read and respond to John's "posts" on the Two Plus Two Forums (www.twoplustwo.com). Away from poker John enjoys spending time with his wife, Nanci, and two young daughters, Olivia and Blythe.

Acknowledgments

I would like to thank Mason Malmuth for providing me with the opportunity to bring this work to poker players everywhere. His confidence in my ability to produce something of value has been an important source of support as I have completed this project. In addition, Mason's writings have influenced me both as a player and a writer. From an early point in my poker career I was fascinated by his topic choices, and educated by the content of his works. *Poker Essays* and *Poker Essays, Volume II* helped inspire me to write this book and his feedback on the material here has, in turn, strengthened this work.

I would also like to express my appreciation to David Sklansky. His teachings have played a central role in my development as a player, and have nudged me to think more clearly about diverse topics. Though my direct consultations with David have been sporadic, the impact of his teaching and written work has made him something of a mentor to me. I am therefore, especially pleased that he agreed to consult on this book. Whatever you find of quality in these pages owes much indeed to David Sklansky.

Thanks go as well to the many friends with whom I have discussed poker over the years, including those with whom I have communicated most recently via e-mail. Talking poker with others seriously committed to learning and sharing knowledge has been invaluable.

I owe a debt of thanks (but certainly not money) to a group of poker players. They number roughly ten or fifteen, and are the toughest players in the San Diego area. I will not name them and risk slighting someone by omission, but they know who they are. Little of the money I have won, but much of my education in poker, has come from them.

I'd also like to thank the many regular participants on the Two Plus Two Forums (www.twoplustwo.com) as well.

x Acknowledgments

Discussing poker over the Internet with players from around the world has sharpened my thinking, and given me a window into the minds of players who think about the game as seriously as they play it.

Thanks as well to June Field and *Poker Digest* who first presented some of this material to a wide audience. I appreciate it.

I need to thank Donna Harris for her meticulous proof reading, and Dave Clint for his cover design and artwork throughout this book.

Finally, special appreciation goes to my wife and children. My daughters, Olivia and Blythe, have shown patience beyond their years, as I have worked on this book. My wife Nanci has encouraged me and critiqued my writing. Her support from the start has helped this project become a reality.

Introduction

Poker happens in the mind. Chips and cards are incidental. Thinking and making decisions, putting yourself inside your opponents' minds, extracting immediate meaning from a web of ranks and suits and relating it to human behavior — these things are poker. Of course students of the game can and must study the details of card play and the principles of poker, in general terms. Inevitably though, as one sits in a game one engages in these activities "inside the poker mind," and it is they which determine one's success or failure. Because I enjoy and am especially interested in these thought processes, I have tried to make them a central part of this book. They are a primary feature of the "strategic thinking" essays, and appear in varied ways in much of the rest of the material. I try to take the reader inside the mind of the player as he explores the game and negotiates the play of hands.

I have paid attention as well to another dimension within the "poker mind" — the impact of emotion on poker play. Here I have drawn on my background in clinical psychology to try to bring a new level of insight and discussion to the topic. You need not be a helpless victim of a tendency to "tilt." I provide ideas to help overcome such problems. I do point out though, that tilt is a more complex phenomenon than it may at first appear, and that no self-help approach will eliminate it for everyone.

In other essays I simply invite the reader to share what is in my mind as I examine concepts that have been overlooked or under emphasized in the poker literature. I include material because it should educate, expose illusions which deceive players, or in a couple of instances simply because it ought to provide interesting reading.

One of my aims in making this material available to a general readership is to contribute to the growth of poker. This is not particularly altruistic on my part. As a middle and higher limit

1

player I would like to have more games to choose from. I believe, moreover, that some of the remarkable growth of poker in recent years can be attributed to important books which have provided guidance to players wishing to learn the game correctly. Here, a number of Two Plus Two books have led the way. In its own way I hope the book you are holding will help create new players, while encouraging established players to do the thinking necessary in order to move up the limits.

Even though this introduction is being written early in 2000, some of this material has already been the subject of much debate. Certain essays, having appeared in *Poker Digest,* have been questioned and discussed vigorously on the Internet. This pleases me. It tells me that my ideas provoke thought and reaction. As hinted above, one of my purposes in writing this book was to do just that. I am glad but not surprised that the material has stood up well to rigorous questioning. Much thought was put into the essays that follow, drawing on what I know from years of winning poker and countless hours of study of this difficult and complex game. I look forward to further discussion.

Part One

Technical Points

Technical Points

Introduction

Expert poker play draws on multiple diverse areas of knowledge. In this section I touch on several. Some of these essays point to common mistakes. After all, a good portion of knowing how to play well is knowing what *not* to do. It is remarkable how often many fairly good players make silly plays when they should know better. I think sometimes this is because despite being decent players they lack a solid grounding in poker theory. They are therefore able to rationalize doing things that a better informed player would know without doubt were costly. In the essays that focus on these errors I try to provide the logic that shows why they are wrong.

Two essays here touch on what can be learned by observing your opponents. If you combine all such observations, including those that would qualify as tells and those of a more general nature, then certainly some significant chunk of your profits are derived from these observations. I have tried in the essay on tell detectability to quantify what you might earn as a result of specific tells. As you will see, this figure may be a little less than most of us would like to believe.

Playing Too
Many Hands: Part I

This is a simple, obvious topic. It's so obvious in fact, that it's often been overlooked or simply not bothered with by poker writers. But it is quite important; for it accounts for much of the difference in results between typical winning and losing players. So let's take a look.

When I began playing poker, I studied the game, trying from the start to learn how to play correctly. It is extremely difficult for someone just starting out to put together the myriad concepts one must coordinate in order to play well. What I was able to do, however, was to begin to follow, on a rudimentary level, the experts' guidelines for hand selection. I was therefore baffled, at first, by the extremely loose starting requirements shared by so many of the players I encountered in the small limit games. Gradually I came to realize that most of these players simply didn't know what they were doing. Few had put any effort into learning correct play.

What continued to surprise me was the observation that even somewhat better players frequently showed down hands which, if the experts were right, should not be profitable under the circumstances in which they had played them. (I am speaking here primarily of hold 'em, though much of what I say clearly applies to other forms of poker as well.) As I refined my understanding of what hands to play and how to play them under various circumstances, I concluded correctly that these players were, indeed, making repeated errors in hand selection. Moreover, I continued to spot this kind of error as I moved up to the middle limits. It is rampant among middle limit hold 'em players who are a little better than average but far from the top in ability. Though it is less common among the best players, even here there are some players whose only real flaw is playing a little too loose. I believe this is the most common, yet most easily avoided class of error in hold 'em.

The Nature of Hand Selection Errors

Let me be clear, I am not talking about those situations in which the play of typically unprofitable hands becomes justified. It is a fact of poker that, within limits, the more skilled you are, and the less skilled your opponents are, the more you will be able to profit from hands which other players, or players facing tougher competition, should throw away. I am talking about situations, often involving opponents of at least average skill, in which there is no valid rationale for the play of a particular hand. This error takes many forms. Most commonly it involves limping in with a hand that is too weak for the situation. Calling with something like

in an early-middle position in a typical middle limit game is one example. It can also take the form of calling a raise "cold" with an inadequate hand. I frequently see semi-skilled players call an average player's early position raise with a hand like:

At other times it involves an unwarranted raise, often with a hand that probably shouldn't have been played at all. Players who routinely raise with Axs tend to be guilty of this mistake. (Sometimes a raise with Axs is not a hand *selection* error per se, but may be an error in the *play* of the hand. This essay applies to some of these kinds of errors as well.) Another raise of this kind involves the use of overly liberal starting requirements when attempting to steal the blinds. (Hint: Any two will usually *not* do here.) I leave it to the reader to identify further examples of the hand selection errors to which I refer.

But What Could it Really Cost?

Some may question whether playing a few extra hands really costs enough to worry about. After all, is not the edge of one hold 'em hand over another typically quite small before the flop? Is not the real strength of a hand defined by the flop? While there is some truth to these ideas, it is not difficult to show that the cost of hand selection errors is higher than most players realize.

Consider first that in committing these errors players cost themselves money by deviating from an ideal that allows for maximum profit. The top poker writers recommend you play about 15 percent of the hands dealt to you. While deviations from this guideline may be indicated by variations in game conditions and structure, we are told that correct hold 'em play calls *generally* for a fairly close adherence to the "15 percent rule." (Note that "15 percent" means the percentage of hands played *overall*. It does not mean that you play 15 percent in all situations. At times you should play far more, at other times far fewer hands. See Malmuth's *Poker Essays, Volume II* for a thorough discussion of what it means to play "15 percent.") As Sklansky has pointed out (see *Getting the Best of It*), only great players are capable of squeezing a profit out of an additional 10 or 15 percent of their hands. Other players are going to make mistakes with these marginal hands and lose money with them. In fact, Sklansky has argued that most top players who do extend the range of hands they play go too far with it. They would obtain even better results than they do if they simply tightened up a bit. I have known very good players who fit roughly into this category. They play well, but are so "busy," especially before the flop in ring games, as they strain to find every conceivable (but in fact often nonexistent) edge, that they surely cut their earnings significantly.

A simple example demonstrates concretely the cost of hand selection errors. Suppose you are able to earn one big bet per hour in a $15-$30 game. Now suppose you add to your play two seemingly marginal, but actually losing hands, per hour. Now suppose that these additional hands cost you an average of one sixth of a small bet, or $2.50, each time you play one. This means that your inclusion of just two additional hands per hour has cut your hourly rate by nearly 17 percent! What's more, many seemingly marginal hands are going to lose even more than this example suggests. (See Malmuth's *Poker Essays* for more on the dangers of "marginal" hands.)

One can easily envision a scenario in which playing, say, 30 percent of the hands dealt could turn an otherwise winning player into a big loser. In fact, I would contend that this category of error alone prevents many players from winning. It is not uncommon to see players who play reasonably well after the flop, cost themselves so much with their loose starting requirements that they remain "producers" wherever they play.

Another way to appreciate the cost of this error is to consider the differences between serious and minor poker errors. In *Getting the Best of It,* Sklansky provides the definitive discussion of this area of poker theory. Here I want to point out that, among poker errors (such as checking when you should bet, raising when you should fold, etc.) electing to play hands that should be folded is a special case. Generally, the serious errors are those that cost you the pot. The minor ones cost just a bet. So it would seem that playing a hand which you should have mucked is a minor mistake. Unfortunately it's not that simple.

It is true that calling when you should fold can be a relatively minor error. Making an incorrect call on the end, for example, costs you just that bet. (Moreover, it is balanced against the much greater cost of folding on the end when you should call, an error that can cost you the pot.) But calling (or raising) when you should fold in the context of hand selection is a different matter. It is more costly for two reasons. First, hand selection is a decision which comes up unusually often (i.e., every hand). Thus, if you consistently make poor decisions here, you are *frequently* costing yourself money. This, of course adds up. Second, mistakes in hand selection tend to compound themselves. For example, a hand which is slightly inadequate for your position can easily turn into a second best hand on the flop. If you do not play expertly enough to recognize what has happened, you are likely to be trapped for several bets against an opponent who may, for instance, have you out-kicked.

If you play extremely well after the flop, you can minimize the compounding problem. Still, it is clear that the frequency problem alone is enough to cut significantly into your hourly rate. It should be obvious that these two factors combined make the cost of improper hand selection prohibitive.

I hope I have made clear that playing too many hands is no minor problem, even for a very skilled player. In Part Two, I will offer some thoughts about what makes so many players — even some very good ones — deviate from sound hand selection.

Playing Too
Many Hands: Part II
Causes and Remedies

In Part I of this examination of overly loose hand selection, I detailed the nature and cost of this obvious but serious problem. Here I will outline some causes of this class of error and suggest some remedies.

What Brings About Too-Loose Play?

Why, given the cost, do so many players, even some very good ones, play hands with a negative expectation? Shouldn't better than average players know that this is a costly practice? Many undoubtedly do, but act counter to their knowledge. Though my ideas about why they do this are conjecture, I believe the answer usually involves one or more of these causes:

1. **Players overrate their abilities.** Some players, after developing a modicum of skill, begin to see themselves as playing somewhere near a world class level. Consequently, having heard that the best players can get away with playing more hands, they think they can do this too. Their overrating their abilities may have to do with the chance element in poker. Because players often win despite flawed play, sometimes for extended streaks, some erroneously associate their results with their play. That they arrive at this faulty conclusion while others don't can result from a lack of knowledge of the fluctuations to be expected in poker. In other cases it has a psychological explanation which is beyond the scope of this essay. Suffice it to say that many people unconsciously seek ways to boost their self-esteem.

For some, deceiving themselves about their abilities in poker provides this boost.

2. **They go subtly "on tilt."** As my essays on the phenomenon of "tilt" explain, I define tilt as the effects of emotional reactions on one's play. I believe the majority of players spend a certain amount of time on tilt without even realizing it. When their misplays are fairly innocuous — a call here, an extra hand played there — they are less likely to identify them as the result of being on tilt. But when you make an error when you know better, that's tilt. It may be a mild instance of tilt, but it is emotion affecting the play of a hand. Your intellect says to do one thing but something makes you do otherwise. That "something" is an emotional reaction, be it frustration, anger, boredom, or nearly any other feeling which becomes strong enough (perhaps unconsciously) to affect your actions. Playing a hand that should be folded, even though you know better, is simply a moment of tilt.

3. **They are influenced by the illusion that any two cards can win.** While this notion is, of course, true in the short term, it is false in the long run. Still, this sense that any two cards can win seems to be so strong in hold 'em that it affects even some of the better players. While they may pay lip service to the importance of selecting the right hands to play, on another level, they don't truly feel it is of much consequence to play a few weak hands, as the flop changes things so much anyway. This illusion is used as a rationalization which facilitates going on tilt.

4. **Intermediate players have gaps in their knowledge.** Players at an "intermediate" level, by definition, have incomplete knowledge about the game. In some cases this is reflected in their understanding of the play of starting hands. Perhaps these players learn other areas of the game before refining their pre-flop play. Though I would suggest to a

beginning player that the first major area to focus on in learning hold 'em (or any other game) is the play of starting hands, some learn instead by circuitous routes.

5. **Some very good players are "instinct" players.** There are players who have become highly skilled at poker without reading books or pursuing formal learning of any kind. They have a good "feel" for the game and have learned by experience, perhaps having stumbled onto a winning approach for a particular game, such as hold 'em. While they may be excellent players overall, their lack of formal learning (reading, studying, analysis, and so on) means that they too will have certain weak areas in their knowledge. Most of the time they will have a fairly good sense of what hands to play, but their standards will be slightly flawed and imprecise, tending to undervalue certain hands while overvaluing others. Such a player may, for example, undervalue a hand like

in unraised, multi-way pots, while overvaluing something like

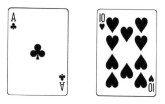

(offsuit) under the same circumstances.

6. **A few skilled players don't play seriously.** There are very few players in this category for a simple reason. I believe that in order to *become* a good player you have to play seriously during a prolonged learning period. Thus, someone in this category would have to have been a serious player, and then, for some reason *stopped* playing seriously. Given the number of people who play poker this probably does occur, but only very rarely. (Note that some good players may try at times to convince themselves and others around them that they are not playing seriously, as a way to rationalize going on tilt. This is a separate phenomenon.)

Are There Remedies?

As I stated in Part One, hand selection errors are avoidable. I have described a number of identifiable causes of such errors. If you find you are prone to such misplays, and are motivated to eliminate them from your game, you may benefit from determining which of the causes I have listed apply in your case. Those that apply will dictate particular remedies.

Cause 1 is tricky to deal with. In the short term your best insurance against overrating your ability is enough education in poker theory to have a sense of how much you actually know. This should be combined with a sound knowledge of the nature of the fluctuations which occur in the game. Study and experience can provide these. Over a longer period of time, however, your results will reflect how well you have played. If you think you have been playing well, yet your results have not been very good, you should consider that you may not be as skilled as you think you are.

Furthermore, if you continue to maintain that you are an excellent player despite contradictory results, it may reflect an emotional problem centering around self-esteem. Moreover, it is a problem which will impact your poker results. If you refuse to believe you are not a great player, you will likely ignore the study and analysis of the game that you need in order to improve.

Without going into psychological detail, I will merely suggest that your best bet for overcoming such a problem might involve psychotherapy. Though entering psychotherapy may sound like an extreme measure, if you are serious about poker and want to earn significant income at the game, you will find, upon doing the math, that it is surprisingly cost effective. It may even save your poker career. (See the essay, "A Poker Player in Therapy.") It is up to you to decide what you are willing to do to improve your play. (You might consider as well the broader benefits you may gain from a well conducted psychotherapy.)

Unfortunately, the need to preserve self esteem tends to be stronger than the willingness to confront oneself honestly. Therefore, most players who do overrate their skill will never acknowledge or even recognize this tendency in themselves. They will not likely seek help until their internal problems create intense distress in other areas of their lives.

Cause 2, going on tilt, can often be remedied without going as far as psychotherapy. Deepening your knowledge of the game so that you develop the "professional attitude" may help a great deal. (See the essays on the topic of tilt.) For some players, going on tilt may be symptomatic of deeper psychological problems. Here again, professional assistance is indicated.

Causes 3, 4, and 5 are addressed through the study of poker. This can include reading, consulting with an expert, and analyzing poker problems and strategies. For the present purpose, study particularly the play of the first two cards, especially *why* certain hands are indicated in certain situations while others are not, and *why* hands are played the way they are.

Dealing with Reason 3, the illusion that any two cards can win, requires the specific development of an understanding of the advantages of one starting hand over another in a given situation. If you almost always defend your big blind, for example, you need a better understanding of the exact nature of the advantages a hand like

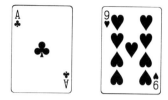

has over something like

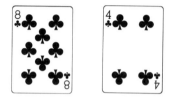

in a heads-up situation.

Cause 6 suggests a scenario in which there is actually no problem to be resolved. If a player is capable of playing consistently well, but for some reason chooses not to, that is his prerogative. I can only wish that the best players in the games I play in would make that choice more often.

It is ironic that an area of hold 'em in which the correct decision is usually pretty simple is also such a common source of errors. I hope that the points outlined here have clarified the cost and causes of these mistakes, while providing some ideas on how to eliminate them from your play.

Bad Plays
Good Players Make

By definition, good players do not make many bad plays in poker. Nevertheless, many good players do have a small number of bad plays that they make routinely. Determining whether or not you have any "pet" bad plays, and eliminating them is an easy way to improve your hourly rate. Here are a few poor plays that seem to be common to at least some good players:

1. **Overuse of the small pair isolation play.** It seems that I used to see this more often in hold 'em games than I do now, but there are certainly still players who are guilty of it. They begin with a play that is actually not so bad if applied very selectively. The play is to three-bet a preflop raiser with a pair like

or smaller. The goal is to get heads-up against the other player, on the assumption that if he does not have a big pair, the holder of the small pair can thus manufacture a small positive expectation. In the right spots this play probably can indeed be slightly profitable. The problem is in using it unselectively.

For this play to be profitable, the situation needs to be right. First, it is crucial that you have a very high probability of successfully isolating the raiser. Yet I have often seen players make the play when the chance that at least one or both blinds would call was fairly high. If you are an experienced player you should see that to invest three bets before the flop with only a small pair, having then to play the hand out in a three or four-handed pot is not an attractive venture. Most (of the 88 percent) of the time that you fail to flop a set, that pair is going to be difficult to play against two or three opponents. (It prefers one, or many opponents.) For example, any combination of overcards on the board and aggression from your opponents will inevitably lead you to make pot-costing mistakes.

To illustrate, say the flop is:

Your two opponents, both average players, check and call your bet. The turn is a

I could have made the turn a K (or a J, or a T, or an A…) but even with this blank, now what do you do when they check again? Are you sure? And what if one bets?

Also important to this play's profitability is that it be applied against the right kind of opponent. The ideal opponent would be one who will raise preflop with a very wide range of hands (such that you are less likely to be up against a big pair), but who will then play tightly, passively, and predictably after the flop (so that you have a good chance of stealing, are not bluffed off your hand, and will know when you can safely fold). While few opponents will fit this profile perfectly, some players will take their small pair and three-bet opponents who do not even come close in one or both qualities. They will try, for instance, to isolate a player who, while loose in his raising standards, is very aggressive after the flop, likely to play back at them unpredictably, forcing them into costly errors. Alternatively, they will make the play against a player who is somewhat predictable after the flop, but whose preflop raising standards are so tight that they run a great risk of clashing with a big pair. Naturally, if you try this play against someone with both high preflop raising standards and a propensity for aggressive, deceptive play after the flop, you are giving up too much in light of this play's marginally positive expectation under the best of circumstances.

On a more general level it is obvious why the small pair isolation play will not have a positive expectation under many typical conditions. A small pair is simply a tenuous little hand when not played almost solely for its set value in a multiway pot. To extract a lot of value from it apart from that derived from flopping sets, is not easy. Yes, it does have value heads-up, and reraising preflop can often make it a heads-up contest. But it does so at a cost of three bets — a price which requires you to make considerably more profit on the hand than that associated with its set value alone in heads-up pots. (To profit from playing it for its set value alone, you would have to average winning more than 20 additional small bets after the flop. That is more than twice what you could realistically expect on the occasions your opponent happens to have an overpair, or to flop one or two pair. You'll make even less when you flop a set but he flops nothing.) The only way you can possibly extract all that extra value is to make the play only selectively, under favorable conditions. To make it indiscriminately is asking too much of a small pair.

By the way, much of what I have just outlined could be said as well about players routinely, and indiscriminately three-betting preflop with medium pairs. This is even more common than the small pair play. But it's not as often, and not as pronounced, an error.

2. **Indiscriminate semi-bluffing against calling stations.** Any reasonably good player has learned the value of the semi-bluff. But some apply it indiscriminately. Usually these are either very aggressive players who have trouble backing down a little when they need to, or mediocre players who have hit on semi-bluffing as a useful ploy, but have little else in their repertoires. Sometimes they are simply players who play a very formulaic game with little ability to make situational adjustments.

As Sklansky points out in *The Theory of Poker*, profit from the semi-bluff comes from the *combined* possibilities that your opponent will fold immediately or, if he does not, you will make your hand on the next card. If your opponent is sure or almost sure to call, the semi-bluff is no longer profitable.[1] Yet I see knowledgeable players reflexively semi-bluff into calling stations all the time. It is almost comical sometimes to see a passive, wholly unskilled player unwittingly outplay a normally solid, aggressive player simply by calling. The aggressive player hangs himself in his own noose as he tries repeatedly, and futilely, to bet the passive player off his hand. Now, this is not to say that you should never semi-bluff against a loose caller, but to do so automatically, without picking your spots, is going to cost you.

---

[1] This isn't always true in stud games. Here it can occasionally occur that a semi-bluff is correct even if you know you will be called in order to get your opponent to fold later on if you happen to catch a threatening card.

3. **Semi-bluffing into a sure raise.** This is another tendency of some players who play too rigidly without adjusting to different opponents and situations. Say a player is in the big blind holding a hand like:

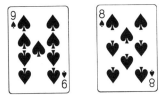

A tight aggressive player opens for a raise under the gun. Another aggressive player, also with reasonably tight starting standards calls in a middle position, as does an average player on the button. Now our player in the big blind decides to call.

The flop comes:

You will frequently see the player in the blind bet out with his flush draw here. As in No. 2 two above, he overlooks the fact that in order for the bet to be right there must be some reasonable chance that everyone will fold to his bet. In this scenario, not only is there little chance all three opponents will fold, but there is an incredibly strong chance the bettor will be raised by one of the aggressive players, knocking out one or two players who might otherwise pay off his flush if he hits it on a subsequent round. After all, the flop contains the kinds of cards the tight, aggressive player would raise with in early position. They are also around the ranks of cards with which the other tight player would likely call a raise cold (though such a player would probably more often reraise). Moreover, there are not really enough opponents to justify betting based on the multiway action you expect to get for your draw. A bettor here will probably end up heads-up, having to call a raise. By betting he is simply putting in more money as an underdog.

Perhaps the main reason players who should know better still make this error is that it doesn't *feel* very costly. Sometimes, of course, he wins the pot, despite his poor play. But even while he's still at the flop he does not really feel punished for the error because he knows he still has a reasonable chance to draw out, and so has an easy call of the raise. If you do the math, however, you will see that the cost to you for making this ill-advised semi-bluff truly lessens your hourly rate.

I should note that this play can actually be correct against a different kind of opponent. If you are up against someone who is extremely "weak tight," then it might be the right move. That is, if your opponent is unlikely to semi-bluff raise, and will readily lay down a hand when he does not connect solidly with the flop, then the benefits of semi-bluffing yourself have increased. Against such a player, however, you might get a free card if you check and he has missed the flop. (Then you can semi-bluff the next round.) You should take this into consideration before deciding what to do.

4. **Trying, with garbage hands, to steal the blinds of skilled, aggressive players, or mediocre, tenacious callers.** When better players make this mistake it is often the result of an inaccurate judgement. They misjudge either the long run profit to be made from attempting to steal a tight, but skilled player's blind, or the edge they posses over a mediocre tenacious caller, despite their weak hand.

When you try to steal an expert player's blind you will probably find that you succeed more often than you do against weak players. This is because weak players tend to defend their blinds too liberally. But the question you should ask yourself is whether, over many steal attempts with weak hands such as

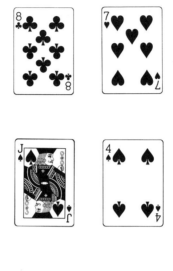

and

you have a positive expectation (i.e., you will profit) against the expert. The problem you may run into is that the occasions when the expert does defend will cost you more than the blinds you successfully steal from him. When he defends, his starting hand will often be better than yours, he will make few errors, and may consistently outplay you. If this is so, then trying to steal his blinds with marginal hands is going to cost you money. My observation is that some reasonably good players do not seem to have thought this through.

When you try with very weak hands to steal the blind of a mediocre player who will almost always defend, the situation is different. The problem here is that unless he plays very badly after the flop, such that your edge on him is then quite pronounced, you are lowering your overall expectation by investing two bets in your below average starting hands. You would be better off simply limping with some of the weaker hands that you deem strong enough to play against him.[2] When you factor in a similarly tenacious small blind who will often call as well, you need to increase your starting standards and raise even less. By constantly raising the blinds of such players you merely dilute your profits. Notice as well, that by demonstrating to such players that you are completely unselective in your steal attempts you reinforce their conviction to defend every time. If you are a little more selective, they may decide to defend less often, an outcome you prefer with most of the weaker blind stealing hands.

5. **Playing sub-marginal hands.** It's true that in hold 'em, the better you get, the more hands you can play — *up to a point.* (And that point may come sooner in hold 'em than in some other forms of poker.) But many good players carry this too far, especially against average or better opposition. They begin to raise out of position with hands like:

---

[2] These are basically hands like Q5s or T8s — hands that will usually not flop anything but ought to make decent money against poor players when they do.

or to call in late position with hands like:

Out of the big blind, they may raise several limpers with a hand like:

For great players all these plays may be correct against terribly weak opponents, but are likely to shade into the zone of negative expectation for anyone less expert, or against better opposition.

Some players are especially prone to start playing such inadequate hands when they've had a winning streak. If the streak happens to continue as they add weaker hands to their repertoire, they can get into a losing habit that costs them a lot of money before they identify the problem.

Many better players fail to understand what is really implied by the idea that as your skill level increases you can play more hands. First, you cannot do as much of this if the opposition is at all tough. Second, you are almost sure to cost yourself money if you try to play these additional hands from early positions. They are mostly just some possibilities to consider for later positions, under favorable conditions. I have occasionally seen otherwise good players try to open for a raise with something like

with four or five people still to act behind them.[3] In typical middle limit games this is suicide. Third, good players usually think they are better than they actually are. In fact, they usually are *not* expert enough to be adding additional hands. When they do, they tend to get into trouble with them. When the true expert plays these hands, a major part of his superior play with them involves his correct folds after the flop, when others would play on. Put differently, he manages to stay out of trouble.

(Note: At the time I am writing this essay, I occasionally have in my regular game a fellow who is a prime example of a player with this problem. His overall playing skills are a little better than average. But he apparently believes he can successfully play many hands that are, in fact, clearly unprofitable. In his case this appears to stem from an arrogant, inflated self image. I suppose he thinks, "I can outplay everyone so totally after the flop that I can play these hands that other good, but not great, players would never dream of playing." As just one example, I recently saw him open for a raise with

---

[3] Sometimes you will see an expert make a play like this. In this case it may be correct if he has noticed that a couple of the players who act after him are already passing out of turn.

with four or five players still to act behind him. Unless he develops some insight into what he's doing, I predict a short and costly poker career for this player.)

6. **Playing an occasional garbage hand out of frustration or boredom.** This is a bit different from the problem described above. Here we have players playing hands they *know* are not profitable. This is not the occasional play of a subpar hand for purposes of deception, with the hope of influencing opponents' future perceptions. They do it because they haven't played a hand in a long time and so are "bored," or because they are frustrated as a result of losing some hands (i.e., they are on tilt).[4] They rationalize it, thinking they can "get away with it" as long as they only do it on occasion. A typical hand used for this purpose is Ax. But a losing hand is a losing hand.

7. **Habitually continuing semi-bluffs past the flop.** In *Hold 'em Poker for Advanced Players: 21st Century Edition,* Sklansky and Malmuth make a good case for often refraining from continuing your semi-bluffs past the flop. They make two good points:
    A. If you always continue the semi-bluff, players will catch on to what you're doing and will begin to bluff or semi-bluff raise you on the turn, and
    B. If you check-raise frequently on the turn with your legitimate hands, then on those occasions when you are checking only because you gave up on a semi-bluff,

---

[4] The "boredom" excuse makes little sense. When you are not playing hands there is more information from which to learn available to you than you can possibly hope to absorb. If you are not going to attend to it, you might as well fight your boredom by reading a newspaper. That will cost you, but not as much as playing silly hands.

your observant opponents will often check along, giving you a free card.

Just about all good players have read Sklansky and Malmuth's book, yet many *habitually* continue their semi-bluffs on through fourth street and then totally bluff on the river. I'm not talking about simply betting again on the turn more often than not — a strategy which I believe may actually be profitable in many games — but about betting nearly every time in all games. So what's going on? I believe it's just that most players are tempted by the prospect of short term gratification. They know that by betting again on the turn they have another chance to pick up the pot. So they go for it, ignoring what their play may cost them in the long run, both as a result of opponents learning to play back at them, and because they have not set up the profitable pattern involving checking on the turn that Sklansky and Malmuth describe.

8. **Becoming Calling Stations.** This may result from someone's having played a good deal in tough, aggressive games. In those games pots tend to become heads-up quickly, and it's common to see players constantly trying to bet one another off the pot with bluffs and semi-bluffs. To survive in such games you have to learn to pick off bluffs, calling (or raising) fairly often with hands you would muck against other kinds of players. But I sometimes see players who have adapted to these games display a pronounced inability to lay a hand down in more average games. They seem always to suspect bluffs and stick tenaciously in pots where the action from their current opponents, unlike those they've become used to, should tell them that their hand is hopeless.

Ironically then, these are fairly good players who pay off generously. Just don't try to bluff them. Since they are good players though, they may adjust and pay off less routinely when they increase their time spent in less aggressive games. *That's* when you can start to bluff them!

Some of the above involve plays which are right under some circumstances or against some opponents, but which turn into losers when done habitually. Be careful about anything you do habitually in poker. The correct play is usually so situationally dependent, that anything habitual is suspect. Watch for habitual plays in your own repertoire, and make sure you are not using them in the wrong places.

Other plays above are simply misguided. They stem from the failure to analyze fully various elements of play. Make sure you think through and can cite logical reasons for everything you do in poker. As a good player you don't want to be caught making bad plays.

Self-Weighting Cold Calls

One of the most frequent and, in my view, most egregious errors I see made, even by players who are somewhat better than average, is that of cold calling other players' preflop raises with inadequate hands. Sklansky and other writers have noted a basic principle of poker which states that, on average, you need a better hand to call a raise than you need to raise with yourself.[5] There are a few reasons for this. First, when you are the first player in, and you come in for a raise, you have two ways of winning. You may steal the blinds, or you may win the pot after the flop. But when you call a raise cold, you have only the second way of winning.

A second reason concerns the relative strength of your calling hand and the raiser's hand. If you hold a hand that is near the bottom of the spectrum of hands you would raise with if you were the opener, then what do you make of your hand if you are faced with a raise from a player whose raising standards are similar to your own? On average his hand will fall higher in that same spectrum.

---

[5] The astute reader may note that it is sometimes correct to call a raise with a hand that would seem to be fundamentally weaker than the raiser's hand. Calling with a small pair in late position after someone has raised and several players have called the two bets is an example of such a call. Note, however, that the value of the small pair is magnified in this multiway situation. In fact, were the pot not already raised, raising with the small pair in this spot could be correct. It has, in effect, become a raising hand. Therefore I see this call (and others like it) as only a *partial* exception to the general principle I am addressing. In the case of these calls, considerations of pot odds and implied odds take on unusual weight and make correct a call that would be out of the question under other circumstances.

But there's more to this relative strength consideration. As Sklansky points out in his essay, "Why You Lose in a Good Game," in *Getting the Best of It,* the odds you are getting from the pot could sometimes make calling under these conditions marginally correct — *if* you knew the raiser did not hold a big pair. In reality, you must of course factor in big pairs when you consider your opponent's spectrum of raising hands. That leaves you with the notion of calling his raise with what figures to be the worst hand, and possibly a hand that is truly "dominated" by a big pair. Adding the big pair factor to the other two I mentioned tips the scales strongly against the option of calling raises without sufficient hand values.

Yet to see players calling raises cold with hands like

or

is common. These are hands just strong enough to raise with in certain situations. More often they are not even playable. Yet players with poor knowledge of preflop strategy, and how it impacts play after the flop, will call a raise cold with these hands without a moment's hesitation.

In *Gambling Theory and Other Topics,* Mason Malmuth introduced students of gambling theory to the somewhat obscure statistical concept of self-weighting and non-self-weighting strategies. Non-self-weighting strategies are the key to successful gambling in beatable games such as poker. As Malmuth puts it, "Non-self-weighting strategies attempt to identify where the gambler has the best of it and then make the most of it." The player following a non-self-weighting approach is very selective in looking only for those situations where he has a positive expectation. When he finds one he then invests (bets) heavily. He will try completely to avoid situations where he lacks a positive expectation. At the very least he keeps his investment in such situations to a minimum. A tight but aggressive style of play reflects this strategy. This of course is the style of nearly all winning poker players.

On the other hand, a player who is not selective about where he invests (bets), and who tends to invest a similar amount in all situations, is following a self-weighting strategy. Part of the problem with such an approach is that any correct, profitable bets that are made tend to be offset by incorrect, losing bets. A loose, passive style is a good example of such a strategy.

Notice what happens if you do everything else correctly, but you call raises cold with hands like K♦J♣. To the pool of all your profitable investments you have added a group of losing investments. The profit from the correct calls and raises you make with something like K♦J♣ is diluted by the cost of incorrect cold calls made with the same hand. Your cold calls represent a self-weighting feature of your play, and cut into the profit you could otherwise make.

I would contend that these cold calls are even more costly errors than might first be apparent. This is partly because they are errors in hand selection, a decision which must be made over and over. Just as importantly, hand selection errors tend to compound themselves as players get into trouble with hands that present difficult decisions after the flop. Moreover, these cold calls are among the *most* costly hand selection errors. Each such misplay, even before it compounds itself, begins with a misguided investment of not just one, but two or more bets.

If someone asked you, "Would you like to find some losing situations and then invest heavily in them?" You would, of course, dismiss the idea as ridiculous. Yet this is precisely what players are doing when they make these self-weighting cold calls. Though they may be selective in the rest of their preflop play, their results are sullied by these horrible calls. While some of these players simply lack knowledge in the fundamentals, those who would seem to know better probably lack the ability to lay down a hand that looks better than average. They fail truly to appreciate that a hand which may be relatively strong in some situations can be a big dog in others.

Of course, I don't mind having these players in my game. Though it can be frustrating to raise with

get called by and subsequently lose to

every time I raise with a big pair and get a call from someone who I know makes this kind of error, I smile a little inside.

Do You Pass
the Ace-Queen Test?

What do you do with

when someone ahead of you has raised in an early or early-middle position before the flop? Do you always play it, usually by calling the two bets cold? Then get into my game please. Most of the time, playing AQ this way is, in my opinion, just one more sign of an unschooled player who is going to be mediocre at best in his overall play.

To see why this is so, consider Sklansky's well known hand groups. Which groups comprise the spectrum of hands a solid player will typically raise with from early and early-middle positions? Of course it depends on the situation (including whether or not anyone has limped in yet, the kinds of players behind him, his current image, and more), but here is a rough, general answer: From an early position he is going to raise with Groups One and Two, and sometimes Group Three. From an early-middle position he will raise with Groups One through Three, and sometimes with certain Group Four hands. Now where does AQ fall in this spectrum? It's at the end of Group Three. That's near the bottom of the list of hands a decent player is going to raise with. Thus, if you call his raise with AQ you are calling with a hand that falls well below the average hand he will be holding.

You might reasonably argue that AQ should actually fair quite well against the other Group Three hands and a couple of the Group Two hands. But that is only clearly true when the pot is not going to be multiway. Here I am addressing the full range of preflop situations. (Even if you were to juggle hands around in the groups to reflect only their heads-up values — for example, promoting AQ to the end of Group Two, and demoting KQs to Group Three — then counting card combinations in Groups One through Three, the AQ is clearly superior to only about 28 percent of the hand combinations that it would go up against.) Even more important is the fact that many good players raise with most of the Group Three hands only a minority of the time in earlier positions. Clearly, you are a big dog holding AQ when a solid player raises in this situation. Note too that many mediocre and weaker players have similar or even tighter raising standards.

This does not mean that AQ is never playable against a raise. Sometimes it is. Among the factors which bear on your decision are your position and that of your opponent, his likelihood of being on a steal or semi-steal, his raising standards, and your opponents' skill level. It is clear, however, that under routine conditions AQ should be folded when it is two bets to you before the flop.

There are lots of ways of making a quick assessment of an unfamiliar player's skill and knowledge of the game. Looking at how he handles AQ when faced with a raise is not a bad little test.

Conjecture on the
Limits of Tell Detectability

Reading tells is fun. Spotting a useful tell in an opponent's behavior and making profitable use of your discovery engenders a secret little sense of victory. It is not entirely clear, however, just how profitable reading tells can be. Mike Caro and Mason Malmuth have debated this point in the poker literature, with Caro asserting that reading tells can provide a major portion of a good player's income, and Malmuth countering that it accounts for only about $2 per hour for an expert in a $20-$40 game (See "The Value of Tells and Positive Reinforcement" in *Poker Essays, Volume II*). My own opinion has been similar to Malmuth's. I have long believed that tells, account for far less profit than such factors as correct strategy and conventional hand reading. Yet most of us do have room for improvement in our ability to identify tells. My purpose in this essay is to examine what might be possible as we approach our limits in this ability.

Mike Caro is the author of the major reference on tells, *The Body Language of Poker: Mike Caro's Book of Tells*. In it he focuses on common tells, exhibited by relatively many players. The tells he describes certainly occur in lots of games, but are more common in the small limits. At the middle limits, where you will find many more decent players, obvious tells such as those involving acting weak when strong, or a player's hand shaking when he holds a monster hand, do not occur as frequently. You do see them, but I do not believe that it is often enough to have a tremendous impact on your hourly rate. Somewhat more frequent are tells such as a player double checking his hole cards or giving away information by beginning to act out of turn.

In addition, I have sometimes been able to spot tells of the more individualized sort. These are the inadvertent mannerisms, movements, and the like, with which some players give away the strength of their hand. Caro mentions only a few of these in his work, perhaps because they often involve the idiosyncrasies of individual players, and so cannot be discussed in general terms. You may find such a tell in one person's play, but see it in no one else's over years at the tables. Such tells are thus difficult to find because you don't know ahead of time what you are looking for. It may be a twitch, a posture, a laugh, a distinct betting motion, or any of countless other possibilities.

Hidden Potential in Subtle Tells?

Nevertheless, I believe there may be some untapped potential in this area of tells. To illustrate what could conceivably be possible let us consider a very good $10-$20 hold 'em player who earns $20 per hour. Let us also assume that he is average (among expert players) in his ability to read tells. Now, just to provide a starting point let's do a very simplistic analysis of what tells contribute to his "earn." In the absence of formal research on this topic, let's just estimate that he identifies and profits from one tell for every seven hours of play. (Some readers will think this sounds like a player who spots few tells. But note that I am crediting those tells with earning whole bets and pots rather than the fractions of bets and pots that could be attributed to them in reality. Thus, this should more than compensate for the reduction in earn created by assuming relatively infrequent detection of tells.) On a given occasion a tell may help him win a bet, save a bet, or win the pot. Rather arbitrarily, I'll say that every 25th tell wins him the whole pot. (Again, in reality it would be more accurate to say that some larger percentage of tells he spots *contribute* to his winning the whole pot, but that would take us into an analysis more complex than is necessary for our purposes here.) Furthermore, I'll say the average pot he then wins consists of 10 betting units ($100 in a $10-$20 game). Finally, I'll say that half the bets he wins or saves by way of the other 24 out of 25 tells are $10 bets and half are $20 bets. Thus, taking $15 as the average bet won or saved by a tell, we see that for 25 tells he earns $460.

$$\$460 \ = \ (24*\$15) + \$100$$

Since each of the 25 tells involves seven hours of play for a total of 175 hours, we divide 460 by 175 to arrive at $2.63 per hour that tells earn this player.

$$\$2.63 \ = \ \frac{\$460}{175}$$

(This is a little higher than Malmuth's figure, but note that he actually allowed for a small *range*, depending, for example, on how much a player *relies* on tells versus card reading, which will often lead to the same decision.)

Now consider that if our expert could *triple* the number of tells he spots, he would earn $7.89 per hour (or $5.26 more than before) as a result of tells, increasing his hourly rate to about $25 per hour. While that's not an astronomical increase it is a noteworthy percentage increase for this player.

But the big question is whether there is any way a player could acquire the ability to identify several times more tells than the average expert at a given limit. The answer is a qualified "maybe, but don't hold your breath." My experience does suggest that there are many tells which are easy to overlook. To support this contention I will first describe a routine hand I played, which involved detecting a simple tell. As you will see, this "tell" was of such an unremarkable nature that some players might not even consider it a tell at all. But if we define a tell as any observable behavior which betrays something about an opponent's hand, then this example is a tell. Its importance, however, is in what it may suggest about the potential to detect other tells which, for most of us, go by unnoticed.

In this hand I had opened for a raise in a $20-$40 game, in a late middle position, holding

Only the big blind called. I had seen her play for only about an hour, but it was enough to know that she played weakly and could have nearly anything. Perhaps only a complete garbage hand could be tentatively ruled out. The flop came

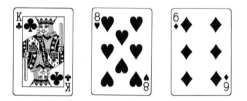

My opponent checked and called my bet. I could not do much to narrow down her hand. She could have certainly had top or middle pair, or could be on a straight draw. The turn was the

and had the same action. The river was the

Again she checked. There was no flush threat, but I had to wonder about a straight or two pair. She had been calling with *something*. Was there a chance she had slowplayed a 9-7 on the turn? Had she made a gut shot with 7-4, or some kind of two pair on the river? Though I had not seen her play enough to know if she had any tendency to check-raise, I knew that if she had a straight that would almost certainly be her action. Unless I had reason to suspect the straight, I wanted to bet for value. Though she could be timidly checking two pair, I believed that she would call me down with any pair, making the value bet a profitable play.

Now, there are occasions when you can pick up a sign that an opponent is planning to check-raise. (If you observe, you will find that sometimes even good players do act in some subtly different ways when their check precedes a raise versus those times it does not. Of course it is also common for unsophisticated players to put on an act and pretend they're thinking about betting, then check, trying to stop their opponents from betting.) But in this instance I thought there was evidence that she was *not* going to raise if I bet. As I observed her check, her action struck me as very genuinely devoid of any ulterior motive. I suppose I saw a sort of unstudied casualness in the way she checked and waited for me to act. Also, I knew that this was an unsophisticated opponent, and therefore guessed that were she to plan a check-raise, she would likely make a more noticeable effort to convince me that she did not have a hand and was not going to raise. It turned out that I was right and was able to collect another bet in the hand. (Had her action been neutral and unreadable, I still probably would have bet; the tell simply allowed me to do so more confidently.)

Behavioral deductions of this sort are so routine in poker that they may not even be included in discussions of tells. I believe most players would see them simply as a given, a response to a little part of the vast background of information which a player processes almost unconsciously during the play of any hand. (e.g., in the scenario above, involving the $10-$20 player, I would have to attribute a larger portion of his profits to reading of tells if I were to include such routine observations. As I outlined it, the scenario refers to the less frequent, more pronounced behaviors most players think of as tells.) Yet my detection of the tell above was, in a certain way, sophisticated. Moreover, it points to an area of tell play which may have some untapped potential for profit.

My observation was sophisticated in that it involved the detection and interpretation of relatively subtle behaviors. My opponent did not exhibit any discreet, conspicuous behavior which constituted a tell. Instead she betrayed the strength of her hand through a bit of demeanor, perhaps in part a posture or facial expression which was different in only slight ways from how she might act with a stronger hand. More precisely, she betrayed her own thoughts or knowledge through her external behavior. ("I don't have much of a hand. I'll just check and call.") This raises an important question. Given that players sometimes betray their thoughts or feelings through subtle but observable behavior, how many more such tells might one learn to detect?

If one were to sit at a poker table and do nothing for several hours a day, for several weeks, but look for tells in the subtle actions of one or maybe two players, I would guess that two things would happen: First, one would identify some useful tells. Second, one would become better at finding tells. But few of us invest this kind of time and effort in spotting tells. There are other aspects of the game which require our attention. In addition, it gets boring watching someone intently, usually discovering nothing of interest over long stretches of time. Ultimately — and usually pretty quickly — we are lured back to participating in a conversation, thinking about some other point of play, or maybe just daydreaming. Indeed, if you spend all your time between hands looking for tells, your hourly rate will suffer, for you will have neglected everything else which requires your attention as a player (e.g., assessing the strategic approaches used by different players, thinking through the play of a recent hand, determining what adjustments to make in response to gaining or losing players, considering how your opponents are perceiving your play, and countless other factors.)

Thus, I do not suggest that you go out and do nothing but look for tells in your future poker sessions. Nevertheless, there are more tells out there than most players realize, requiring only disciplined observation to uncover. Furthermore, practice should improve one's skill in this endeavor. Eventually one might become able to spot more tells, with more ease in many opponents. For instance, given that I was able to detect that my opponent was not planning a check-raise, might it not be possible to detect the same thing, perhaps through *more* subtle behaviors, in more sophisticated opponents? This seems at least plausible. If one could do it, one could certainly win or save more bets.

Evidence for the Detectability of Very Subtle Tells?

Though much of what I have said is conjecture, I do have a bit of evidence that such enhanced tell reading may be possible. First, I have noticed that my own ability to find tells has improved perceptibly during periods when I have increased my focus on this area of play.

More intriguing is the possible implication of something I saw on television some years ago. The program was one of the genre featuring unexplained phenomena, unsolved mysteries, and other oddities. Though I do not remember the details, featured in this episode was an elderly man from another country. He had an act which people viewed as a demonstration of a sort of psychic phenomenon. He did not, however, claim to posses any psychic abilities. In his act he left the theater, then had someone known to have no connection with him hide a small object, perhaps a coin or a paper clip, with an audience member chosen by the hider. On his return the performer strolled through the audience, holding the arm of the hider. He observed the audience, looking here and there, stopping momentarily, then moving on. Finally he stopped and pointed to the person with whom the object had been hidden. He had found the object by some unidentified means.

Of course this would be unremarkable were it likely to have been only a magician's trick. There are undoubtedly ways a sophisticated magician could arrange a routine of this sort. What made it remarkable was that it was witnessed and assessed carefully by James Randi. Randi, or "The Amazing Randi" is well known as a magician turned preeminent debunker of claims of psychic abilities. Among other accomplishments, he exposed famed "psychic" Uri Geller who, at the time had created a stir with feats like "psychic" spoon bending. Randi even received a MacArthur foundation grant to continue his debunking work. In this instance he observed the act in detail, and was, I believe, privy to the performer's activities before the act, outside the theater, and so on.

What was his assessment of this performers act? Not surprisingly he confirmed that it involved no psychic phenomena. Less expected was his assertion that it also was not a trick! Randi stated that the performer had apparently practiced reading people's subtle bodily cues to such a degree that he had become able to use the cues of the hider and audience members to zero in on the member with the hidden object.

If Randi was right, then we have something of interest to poker players. Could it be possible to learn to detect remarkably inconspicuous tells in our opponents? I have little doubt that it is possible to identify tells more effectively than the great majority of poker pros. But I am less certain that the difference could be enough to make a substantial improvement in hourly rate. Tripling the number of useful tells you identify — especially if you are already somewhat skilled in this area — may be asking too much. Just what the limits of tell detectability are I do not know. I do know that I have not run across any players who clearly read tells vastly better than most other professional level players.

Ultimately a serious player must keep in mind that poker is a multifaceted game. Few players could not improve significantly in several areas of play. So while there may be untapped potential in tell play, you must consider the equal or greater value of numerous other skills. You will then be in a position to prioritize the areas in which improvement will bring you the greatest profits.

Addendum: Not long after writing this essay, while reading a book of stories from the life of the late physicist Richard Feynman, I came across a description of what appears to be nearly the same performer's routine described above. Feynman's father did some investigating to learn the secret of the act. It turns out that it does involve reading the subtle cues of the hider. The interesting thing is that it apparently does not require much practice to learn how to do this. You just need to know what kind of cues to look for. This is consistent with what I have experienced in reading tells. They can be hard to uncover, but once you spot one it becomes almost obvious, and is easy to see again in the future.

Quick Indicators

To do well at poker you need to be able to accurately assess your opponents' play. The first step in this task is usually to gather some evidence concerning their general level of expertise. Naturally, it behooves you to be able to do this quickly. The ability to do this actually comes with minimal effort as you develop enough knowledge of poker to recognize opponents' mistakes. But to help you on your way, I'll outline some tip-offs in hold 'em that better players look for as indicators of an unfamiliar opponent's general level of skill. This should provide not only a look into one small area of the thinking of a skilled player as he plays, but also some items you can begin to monitor in your own game to see how you measure up. If you see in your own play any of the tip-offs of the "unschooled" player, it may suggest that your game needs some work. With one exception, the indicators I provide are elements of play. There are of course more superficial indicators to be noted in a player's appearance and behavior, but those are of relatively little value since you will know whether or not to discount them after the first few minutes of play.

1.   **What do his cold calls tell you?** One hallmark of the "unschooled" player is the tendency to call raises cold more often than the best players do. In general, you need a very good hand to play against a cold raise — a better hand, in fact, than you need to raise with. Under typical circumstances these hands are usually good enough to reraise with. And in fact, this is just how better players most often play them. Now, there are certain hands with which it more often does make sense just to call a raise. There are also situations in which you should just call with the usual reraising hands. But watch a number of expert players and look at what they do when they decide to play a hand against a raise. Most of the

time you'll see them reraise. Moreover, when they observe a player who more often calls raises cold it's a serious tip-off to them that he will likely be weak or mediocre in his play.

I will point out that there are little pockets of theory, subscribed to by knowledgeable players, which advocate just calling raises more often than this. But you will run into these players fairly rarely. They are exceptions. So rather than debate the merits of such an approach, I simply want to point out that, statistically speaking, this aspect of play can be the basis for a good initial guess as to how well a new opponent is likely to play.

Note too that if you actually get the chance to see a preflop cold caller's cards, you'll have even clearer information. If you see that he's calling raises cold with hands he should reraise with, that's bad enough. But if he's calling with hands like

or

that's another (very large) step down the ladder in his apparent understanding of the game.

2. **Does he demonstrate a sensitivity to position?** A skilled hold 'em player will play far more tightly early than he does

in later positions. On the other hand, many weaker players play as if oblivious to position. They'll play a

as easily under the gun as they will on the button because "It's two big cards for heavens sake!" Pay particular attention to what he shows down from early positions. There are really only a small number of hands that are profitable from these spots, so it stands out clearly when you see a player repeatedly show down hands that no one is good enough to profit from in an early position. Be aware, though, that a good player may occasionally play a seemingly goofy hand early just to add mix to his play and induce incorrect reads on the part of his opponents.

3.   **How is his play in the blinds?** One easy-to-spot tip-off of a player's general skill level is whether or not he ever throws a hand away for half a bet in the small blind.[6] If he's not folding some hands here, then he's one of the masses of too-loose players.

Does he habitually defend his big blind when it is raised? Okay, then how about his small blind? Near-habitual small blind defenders virtually always have clear weaknesses in their play, and are usually pretty bad players overall.

4.   **How does he play with regard to the dimensions, "loose/tight" and "passive/aggressive?"** Though correct

---

[6] In games where the small blind is two-thirds of the big blind players who no longer throw away their hand for that extra one-third of a bet are not really doing anything wrong.

play must vary according to the kind of game you are in, better players tend mostly toward a tight, aggressive style of play. For example, if you are sitting in a typical, middle limit game, about average overall in the tightness and aggression of the players involved, and you see enough of an opponent's play to know that he's very loose and aggressive, you can be fairly confident that he is playing less than expertly. More observation is required to determine just how badly he plays, but this simple indicator is a good start.

5. **Can he lay a hand down?** Watch to see if and when he folds over the course of a reasonable number of hands played. (Don't be fooled by a player who has simply run well for a while. Make sure you've seen enough hands to be meaningful. That usually includes seeing some hands shown down.) If he seems to have trouble laying hands down, then you may have found a "calling station." If he's passive, and calls almost habitually, then you're dealing with one of the easiest, most profitable kinds of opponents to have in a game.

6. **Is his play straight forward or does he show signs of deception?** Of course you prefer the straight forward player (unless your opponent is a complete maniac). He bets when he has something, checks when he has little, and raises only with strong hands. His lack of deception simply tells you what kind of hand he has most of the time. To know consistently where you stand in relation to your opponent in a hand is pure profit.

7. **How does he react to "bad beats"?** This is another easy-to-spot indicator. It is the only purely behavioral indicator that I will include in this list. I do so because it is actually fairly reliable. Though there are some skilled players who steam their money off, and many who do grumble a bit after a bad beat, the great majority of the time when you see a player react with intense frustration or disgust, that player turns out

to be mediocre at best. Alternatively, such a player may display these emotions less intensely, but very consistently. But by the time you've seen this, you should have already developed a good line on his play.[7]

The indicators above are but a sampling of the things you can look for to get a quick sense of an opponent's level of play. But they are among the signs I have found to be the most reliable, and easiest to spot.

A quick example: Not long before writing this essay I was playing in a good $40-$80 game one evening when a player I'd never seen before sat down. He seemed fairly aggressive, and was winning about $800 or $900 early on. An acquaintance leaned over and asked me, "Isn't that guy supposed to be some expert on hold 'em? I think I saw him give a talk in L.A. at a poker seminar." I said, "I don't know. Could be. I've never seen him before though." Over the next hour or so, as the player in question lost a few hands, he showed increasing frustration and anger at being drawn out on. It also became clear that he was playing too loosely in general, and defending his blinds with nearly anything, then staying with hands too tenaciously in the face of clear signs that he was beaten. I made a mental note to bet for value a little more liberally versus this player than I would against better players. Within another hour he was down about $2,000, and his play had deteriorated noticeably. Shortly thereafter he got up in disgust, and moved to a $20-$40 game. To this day I have no idea who this person was or if he had in fact given a talk on hold 'em in L.A. But I do know he was no expert, and it didn't take long to determine that and adjust accordingly.

---

[7] This indicator does not hold as reliably in very big games where some good players are known to get quite upset at bad beats. Perhaps this is because they are playing for a significant portion of their net worth.

Technical Points

Afterthought

Notice that many of the mistakes I discussed in this section involved the failure to fold. Though it seems most players do not want to believe it, folding when others would not is a key to winning at poker. Though it does take much more than this to win, especially as you move up the limits, if you consistently make the "calling when you should fold" mistake, which almost always defines the average player, your results too will be no better than average. After reading this section, players who still play too many hands or incorrectly call raises cold will be short on excuses for their actions. Since they *will* know better, their misplays will be attributable only to tilt. That, of course, is the subject of another section.

Tells are, in my view, one of the most fun aspects of poker. Nevertheless, it is difficult to demonstrate logically that a substantial part of one's profits derives from anything other than fundamentally correct play with appropriate situational adjustments, and reading hands and thoughts. I am sure some will disagree with my analysis in the essay on tell detectabilty. That's fine; it was offered not as the last word on the topic, but to stimulate thought and discussion.

Part Two

General Poker Concepts

General Poker Concepts

Introduction

Topics in this section range widely. You will notice, however, that several expose illusions which fool many a player. The players least likely to be fooled are those who have *studied* the game. Some good "instinct" players are surprisingly susceptible to illusions about luck, who the best players are, and the like. Though some illusions of these sorts are not too harmful, failing to see through others will definitely affect how you play. Your earnings will suffer. Strive to be the player of clear, analytical vision, untouched by the illusions into which hordes of players futilely invest so much energy.

Other essays here may help broaden the way you think about poker. I hope that after reading this section, readers who have not thought about it before will be sensitive to issues involved in game preservation. Others may come to see short-handed play in a new, more favorable light. My intent with the essays on how I learned poker is to offer an array of ideas from my own experience which interested readers can draw upon to structure how they work on their game. Finally, though game selection is of paramount importance to winning players, to make good money in poker you must learn to beat games that are a little tougher than those found in the small limits. As simple as this idea is, some portion of players fails to appreciate it. I provide an essay here for those optimists who hope to get rich playing only in "no fold 'em" games.

"The Best Player
I've Ever Seen..."

Nearly any time you hear a poker player begin a story with the line that titles this essay, you should be skeptical. Now, when the person referred to has demonstrated some staying power by maintaining a reputation as a top player (perhaps only in a certain area) for a number of years, or is a well known player, consistently acknowledged as one of the best, then the story may actually have some credibility. Over the years, however, I have heard many stories of this sort about players whom I have never heard of. In no instance that I can think of, did this supposed great player ever emerge to become another Chip Reese or Ray Zee. I have even heard stories like this about players in my own area. They were players who did not frequent the same cardrooms I did, but as they were supposed to be so good, I assumed that I would eventually run across them, or would continue to hear their names mentioned. This has not happened.

So what becomes of these supposed great, though unknown players? To a knowledgeable player the answer should be clear. These stories typically single out someone who plays with a certain style — a style that involves playing lots of hands and playing them very fast. The player described is usually thought to be able to win tremendous amounts of money through extreme aggression and incredible hand reading skills. The problem is that such a fast style is just not characteristic of the great players in live games. Though some forms of poker allow for the play of a few more hands than others, in limit poker, the players who win the most in the long run tend to play with a fundamentally tight, aggressive, but generally prudent style. This is not to say that there are no exceptions. Certainly some of the very best are able to speed around a bit more. But they are very few in number. Moreover, I would argue that those among the top long term money winners who do lean more in this direction are not as loose/fast as many would like to believe. When you read a credible poker author's contention that the best players can play more hands than those less skilled, you should not jump to the conclusion that this means these players sit there and play as many hands as the average player at the table. They don't.[8] They play significantly more than the very tight, unimaginative "rocks," but fewer than the typical unschooled recreational player. Of course they also play them much better.

Players who do play lots of hands with an extremely aggressive style will sometimes have amazing winning streaks. This is to be expected. They play with a highly fluctuating style, so they sometimes have impressive upward fluctuations. These swings can last longer than you might realize, especially when the player is skilled in other areas of the game. But, without exception, reality eventually slaps them in the face. Because their style is fundamentally flawed, their results eventually approach their true expectation — which is not great, and is often ultimately negative.[9]

Thus, the reason you may hear about a player who is supposed to be unbelievably good, only to notice over time that this person never emerges to become better known, even within a limited area, is that the player you heard about is broke and, perhaps, out of the game. This is a common occurrence.

Why do so many poker players point to one of these rather loose, fast players when they try to identify a great player, even the best they've ever seen? I have a little theory about that. I believe that these freewheeling, aggressive players support a wish

---

[8] Mason Malmuth points out that this is especially so in hold 'em. (Poker Digest, Vol. 1, #11, p. 31) He asserts that expert hold 'em play does not allow for as much loosening of starting standards as expert play in some other forms of poker.

[9] For more on essentially the same players see "Sizing Up Those Flashes" in Sklansky's *Poker, Gaming, & Life.*

held by many players. Many players *wish* that it might be possible to play that way and win. They wish that *they* could do it. And when they see someone *appearing* to do it, it gives them hope that just maybe they can. Wouldn't it be fun, after all, to be able to play lots of hands and to run over the games, reading your opponents so well that you win far more than a normal good player's share of pots while avoiding trouble with uncanny consistency? How nice it would be to score big win after big win and achieve hourly rates well in excess of what is supposed to be possible. I think this is what typical players dream of doing. That is their long range goal. If they could never identify anyone who *appeared* to have such abilities, they would have to conclude that maybe their dream was based on fallacious thinking, that maybe it was not a possibility. And that would be a painful loss, a loss of hope. Thus illusory heroes of poker are created in the minds of those whose study of the game has been insufficient.

The Hit and Run Follies

It took me a while to realize how smart they were. I'm talking about the hit and run specialists. How clever, how sensible, and so admirably disciplined are these players! They've really got it figured out. They get ahead by a nice little chunk of money, then … *lock it up*. No need to get greedy. Leave with the money and have a *guaranteed* win for the day. No way to do that if they play on, risking a big downswing. Have you seen the light and joined this knowing crowd? If you do you can increase your percentage of winning sessions dramatically. Now that I have looked closely at how these wise players operate, I can even provide you with a simple rule of thumb to assist you in your hit and run ventures. Always quit a session when you're ahead by nine big bets. When you're losing quit whenever you want to. But *always* quit when you're nine bets ahead for the day. Using this method a lousy player I know has won in 31 of his last 40 sessions — a pretty good record for a bad player.

Yes, it took me a while to realize how smart the hit and run players are: *Not very*. The bad player I know finds it odd that his cumulative results reveal that he has continued to lose money over those 40 sessions. Perhaps I could point out to him that he would win even more often if he quit whenever he had won just five bets. Unfortunately he would continue to lose. But wait, that's not the optimum setting for his system. He could *truly* maximize his winning percentage by always quitting the second he got even one chip ahead. Are you starting to see the folly in all of this?

The important thing the lousy player doesn't realize is that his method of "stop wins" can do nothing to improve his hourly rate. As with all players, and as with you, his hourly rate, multiplied by hours played, is all that really matters. It alone will determine how much he wins or loses over any number of hours played.

It is folly to think you can improve your long run results by even one little speck through any sort of stop win, hitting and running, locking up a win, or whatever you care to call it. It is folly to think you are helping your results by quitting two hours earlier than you need to in a session just because you're ahead by some arbitrary amount of money.

I am not the first to point out the nonsense in stop wins. If you've done your reading, then you've heard this, and seen similar critiques of "money management" ideas from other writers. But, I still see winning players who clearly use a hit and run approach, setting "stop wins" for themselves, or simply by quitting whenever they have put together a modest win. I further see players on poker discussion sites on the Internet continue to espouse the benefits of locking up a win of a certain size. I am therefore compelled to offer my own take on it. I hope I can prompt a few more players to think through the logic of the issue a bit more clearly.

Work on Your Hourly Rate, Not Your Percentage of Wins

Here's the truth: Suppose there were three winning players of differing skill levels. We'll call their abilities "fair," "good," and "very good." I'm sure you will agree that, on average, after a large number of hours played each of these players will have made a different amount of money. Obviously, for each that amount will be a function of his individual skill level. Let's say that they have been playing $20-$40 hold 'em for 1,000 hours. Perhaps the fair player will have made $10,000, the good player $25,000, and the very good player $40,000. Obviously, since their results occurred over time, each player made a certain amount of money *per hour*. So it is easy to see that the fair player made $10 per hour, the good player $25 per hour, and the very good player $40 per hour. Those are their hourly rates. In other words their skill levels are reflected in their hourly rates. Each player plays at a skill level that generates a certain hourly rate. Each player's hourly rate will determine how much he makes over time.

Because the fair player was playing at a skill level adequate to produce $10 per hour, he made $10,000 over 1,000 hours. (Of course this example is hypothetical, and the element of chance dictates that he would not likely have made *exactly* 10,000 dollars. In all likelihood he would have made somewhat more or less. But the result would almost certainly have been somewhere within a statistically identifiable range around that $10,000 mark. Moreover, 1,000 is not an especially large number of hours. A larger number would more surely produce a result which more accurately reflected his skill level. I use 1,000 hours simply to make my point.) Without increasing his skill, (which includes not just the elements of his play, but also his ability to stay off tilt, his skill at game selection, his ability to avoid marathon sessions, and other such factors), there was *nothing* he could have done to insure making more money over those thousand hours. Because he played at a level of skill sufficient to produce exactly $10 per hour, his total profit over a large enough number of hours would inevitably be consistent with that hourly rate.

If you want to make more at poker in the next year you must improve your hourly rate, or put in more hours at your present rate. But stop wins, no matter how you might use them, are not going to help. Of course they won't hurt much either — at least not over a given number of hours.[10] What you make over a given number of hours will be determined by what you are able to make *per* hour, your hourly rate. That is determined by your skill, which remains the same whether you hit and run or not. Note however, that using stop wins will reduce the amount you make during any extended period. This is because repeatedly stopping before you

---

[10] They may hurt a little because quitting early when you are winning often means quitting when you are playing your best and your image is at its most effective, enabling you to win more easily. If you do not play through such periods you miss out on those times when your hourly rate is likely at its highest.

would otherwise means you play fewer total hours. Fewer hours of winning play means less money made.

To be thorough I will mention that there are, in fact, occasions when quitting with a small win can make sense. If the win will break a losing streak, for example, its emotional benefits for you may outweigh other considerations. (Similarly, while the notion of a stop loss [when game conditions are favorable and you are still able to play well] is fallacious as well, you might also choose to wait until you lose a pot or two before you quit a mediocre game that you really don't want to play in but where you happen to be getting lucky, and thus have an intimidation factor temporally working for you.) My purpose here is not to discount this or similar exceptions, but rather to contribute to the debunking of any idea that a money management notion such as the stop win can, in and of itself, actually improve your results over a given number of hours.

The Next Hour You Play...

It all comes down to a fundamental reality: *The next hour you play is the next hour you play.* You can quit now because your chips have reached some arbitrary point. Then you can play your next hour tomorrow, picking up right where you left off. Or you can play your next hour right now.

I should add that while many players are annoyed by those who hit and run, I frequently like seeing them do it. When a good player hits and runs it gets him out of the game, allowing for the possibility that a bad player will take his place. (It also tells me that this guy may not be as good as I think. If he is illogical about this, so may he be about other aspects of the game.) When a bad player hits and runs it slows down his losing. (This is analogous to the winning player making less over a period of time if he uses stop wins. In either case the stop wins simply slow down the inevitable.) But it does help him to come back and play another day. That is usually good for the health of a game. I suppose it is only those players who play near a break even level, who I don't like to see hitting and running. I believe that their keeping a seat filled is probably the best thing they can do for a game.

The next time you are winning and are tempted to quit to "lock it up" even though the game is still good, and even though you had originally planned to quit at a later time, ask yourself what logical reason you have for quitting early. You may find that you are thinking much like the roulette player who bets black because he has seen the ball land on red five times in a row, and so figures it is "due" to land on black. You fear that because you have been winning for a while, you are due to have a downswing. By now you can see that that is just as naive as the roulette player's reasoning. In fact, you are wasting your time even thinking about it. I submit that you will earn more by thinking instead about your play, and that of your opponents. After all, the next hour you play is the next hour you play. Thinking about quitting because you're winning is folly.

An Illusory Winner

Vito had his usual giant stack of chips in front of him that day, and as usual I heard a couple of comments from players who were perplexed, sure that he won consistently, but puzzled about how he did it. As usual they were wrong.

The player I'm calling Vito is someone I used to see frequently in a couple of different Southern California cardrooms. He had a few well developed poker skills. He was aggressive and deceptive, capable of exerting a lot of pressure with semi-bluffs. But he made serious mistakes. He bluffed and semi-bluffed far too frequently in most games. In addition, he played way too many hands, often overplaying them before the flop. It was probably his looseness that nagged at other players when they struggled with their perception that he was a winning player. They knew that winners weren't supposed to play that many hands, yet Vito did and seemed to win consistently — so much so that these other players were even a little intimidated by him. They figured he must know something they didn't. He did; he knew that he was *not* a winner.

A player like Vito is unlikely to keep records of his play. So at times he may have been able to convince himself — as he did others — that he was winning. After all, he did play well enough that he shouldn't lose as heavily as a truly weak player. That combined with a playing style that created big fluctuations led him to have some big wins and, no doubt, some extended winning streaks. So he might sometimes have deceived himself into believing that he'd just had some terrible luck in the past, but was back on track and winning as he should. However, he knew he hadn't won much, and if he was honest with himself he had to admit that he was not winning at all. (He supported himself outside of poker, and had to realize that his overall cash flow has not improved.) Not surprisingly, I don't see Vito around anymore.

Knowledge Fights Illusions

My purpose in this essay is not to disparage Vito or others like him.[11] It is to see what can be learned from the other players' perceptions of him. I believe that their seeing him as a winner, and being intimidated by him, points to an important lesson: *Education in poker theory reduces one's susceptibility to illusions which can interfere with good play.* That is, knowledge of poker theory not only helps you determine the right plays, but helps you avoid misperceptions which can influence your judgement as you play.

The fact is that most players who were familiar with Vito were deceived by the illusion that he was a winning player. Yet you must perceive accurately how well your opponent plays and what mistakes he makes in order to play him correctly. Because these players misperceived Vito's play, failing to see his errors, they were not in a position to play optimally against him. If they did not see that he bluffed *too* much, they would not appreciate the benefits of letting him bet their hands for them more often. If they did not see that he raised too loosely before the flop, often with hands that he should not even have played, they would not think to reraise him sometimes with certain hands which they would fold if faced with a raise from a solid player.

To avoid buying into illusions as Vito's opponents did, we might first look at how they arise. There are three elements which seem clearly to have contributed to the illusion that Vito was a

---

[11] Vito is far from unique in the poker world. Perhaps you have run across similar players who *seem* to win despite violating numerous fundamental principles of sound poker play. Be assured that when they do this, they do *not* beat the game. Be aware also that unless you are a very knowledgeable player you may not always be able to recognize what a top player is or is not doing correctly. You should not automatically assume someone is a "Vito" just because he *seems* to do some things incorrectly.

winner. First, for whatever reasons, Vito went to some lengths to camouflage his losses. He did all he could to *look* like a winner. He stacked his chips so they were difficult to count, was hyper-discreet about buying more chips, and often kept additional chips in his coat pockets which, when his stacks got low, he secretly placed on the table when he believed no one was looking. (How do I know? Well, after noticing repeatedly that his chip stack seemed not to shrink much even after he had lost several pots in close succession, I deduced that he *had* to be doing this. So I watched unobtrusively one day after he had lost over half of his original buy-in. Sure enough, during a hand in which Vito was not involved, just as the dealer spread the flop and all eyes — except mine — were on the community cards, he pulled about ten chips out of his pocket and placed them on the table as smoothly as a magician palms a coin when the audience is looking in the wrong direction. One friend began referring to this routine as Vito's "sprinkling holy water" on his chip stacks, miraculously healing their shrinkage.) The result was that his losses were difficult to detect and his wins appeared bigger than they were.

The second contributing element involved the social pressures inherent in groups — the group around a poker table being no exception. In group situations people are sometimes more likely to express a particular judgement (e.g., judging that a color is bluish versus greenish) if it has been expressed by others around them. This can be true even if the judgement is inaccurate and runs counter to their own first perceptions. That people can be so influenced by a group is fairly common knowledge, almost discernable through common sense. It has also been demonstrated convincingly through experimental research in the area of social psychology. Of course the susceptibility to such influence varies widely depending on the individual and the conditions to which he is subjected. Its relevance here is that such pressures may add to the tendency to assess incorrectly the skills of an opponent. When the general consensus is that a player like Vito is a winner, another player may reason, "Everyone thinks he's a winner; I guess maybe he is."

The most important element in this illusion was that most of his regular opponents lacked sufficient knowledge of poker theory to assess Vito's play on its own merits. They did not have enough poker knowledge to be sure of his mistakes or their severity, so their focus was drawn to fluctuations in his stack size — the wrong data. Because this was an especially deceptive indicator in Vito's case, they readily arrived at incorrect conclusions about his results. Not surprisingly, when I polled a couple of the very *best* players I know, they had no doubt at all that Vito lost at poker. They had the knowledge to know incorrect, unprofitable play when they saw it. In fact, when I asked one of these players what he thought of Vito's ability, he paused for a moment, then chuckled, "If he banks cash at the end of the year, I'll be a monkey's uncle!" If those who see Vito as a winner had done their homework on poker theory, they too would have been unswayed by his deceptive chip practices, and the social pressures at the table. Then they would have seen Vito's play more clearly, and would have played against him more profitably. I suppose it is to Vito's credit that he was able to sell himself as a winner to so many of his opponents. He surely lost less than he would have had they all seen him realistically.

It is a simple test of your poker knowledge to see if you can accurately assess another person's play. If you have learned poker well, you should be able to cite specific reasons why a person is or is not a winning player. Then you will not be deceived by the Vitos of the poker world. You will then play better against them.

On Randomness, Rushes, Hot Seats, and Bad Luck Dealers

Some of the most persistent fallacies in the poker world revolve around notions that the cards fall in predictable patterns. Three of the most common fallacies are:
1. You can be *on* a rush during which you can *expect* better cards than usual.
2. A seat in which a player has been receiving good cards can be expected to continue to receive good cards.
3. Certain dealers can be expected to deal a player especially good or bad cards.

Each of these notions reflects a lack of appreciation of the concept of randomness.[12]

---

[12] To avoid needlessly expanding the scope of this essay I will not address the variations which exist in the definition of "randomness." Some of these variations seem to have come about more for practical purposes of obtaining useful research samples than for their logical precision as definitions of randomness. Here I am conceptualizing randomness as a feature of the sampling *process* (e.g., the shuffle and deal of the cards). It follows — and this essay will elaborate on this — that a set of data (e.g., a series of dealt hands) obtained by a random sampling process may *appear* quite unrandom. That is to be *expected* some of the time. (See *Randomness*, 1998, Chap. 9, by Deborah J. Bennett, for further discussion of this matter.)

A Coin Toss Rush?

One of the simplest ways to illustrate the idea of randomness is the coin toss. I will use coin toss analogies to show the irrationality of each of the fallacious notions I have mentioned. First, consider the idea of being on a rush. Many (perhaps most?) poker players believe that they can identify when they are on a rush. They believe that they can then play substandard hands because, since they are *on* a rush, they will tend to make good hands on the flop or later, at a frequency greater than what could normally be expected.

This is an illusion. To understand why, one must first understand that the cards you receive are random. The cards are scrambled and shuffled to create unpredictable sequences each deal. Now the astute reader might note that a player is more likely to be dealt certain combinations of cards, or to make certain kinds of hands, but this still does not say that the deal of the cards is not random. It means only that the resulting combinations are not equally likely. It is rather like throwing two dice. The outcome is random, though certain numbers are more likely to come up than others. (See e.g., the discussions in the book *Randomness* by Deborah J. Bennett.)

An implication of the randomness of the cards dealt is that you cannot accurately predict what cards you will receive next. You *can* accurately say, for example, that you are more likely to be dealt AK than AA. But you cannot predict better than statistical probability when you will receive one or the other.

But what if you were to pick a period when you happen to have been receiving a highly unusual assortment of cards. Say that for a half hour you happen to have been dealt a far greater than average number of "premium" starting hands such as big pairs, AK, AQs and the like. At that point, can you not predict that you are *especially* likely to receive a premium hand on the next deal? Well, this is a good time to look for enlightenment in a coin toss.

Say you begin to toss a fair coin over and over. Beginning on the 458th toss you happen to have a streak of 17 tails in a row.

Would you be willing to lay odds that it will come up a tail on the next toss? Would you agree to bet, say, two dollars to someone else's one dollar that the next toss will produce a tail? To do so you would have to be convinced that the chance of a tail coming up on the next toss is no longer 50 percent. You would have to believe that it has somehow risen to over 66 percent. Think about that. As you looked at the coin sitting in your hand prior to the next toss, you would actually have to believe that some force was present making it over 66 percent likely to come up a tail.

Let's look at the issue another way. Say you record the results of several million coin tosses in a row. Now you go back and look at the outcomes in sequence. So you have data that could look something like this: TTHTHHHHTHTTTTTTHTH... Now suppose that you pick out 100 sequences within the several million in which the first ten tosses of the sequence produced a head. You don't look beyond the tenth toss of each sequence. Since each of these sequences has least ten heads in a row, is it reasonable to assume that they should, on average, be more likely to show a head on the next toss than would be the case for sequences of, say, three heads in a row? Bear in mind that if you answer yes to this question you must believe that the ten head sequence has caused the coin to change in some way.

The sequence of heads coming up many times in a row is directly analogous to the poker player making many good hands in a row. Unless you believe that for these coin toss sequences the chance of the coin coming up a head on the eleventh toss is greater than 50 percent, you will lack logical consistency if you believe the player who has made many good hands in a row is more likely than normal (i.e. more likely than statistical probability) to make a good hand on the next deal.

Does this mean that rushes don't actually exist? No. Players do sometimes make a high proportion of winning hands over a period of time. My point is simply that you can never accurately say you are *on* a rush or that you are *playing* your rush. You can only say that you have *been* on a rush over some time period in the immediate past. You cannot predict, better than chance, any continuation of that rush. Therefore, to change anything about your strategy based on the notion that you are "on" a rush that you expect to continue is ridiculous. This does not mean that you should never make a strategic adjustment based on having *been* on a rush, and as a result of how you believe your opponents are therefore, responding to you. That is a different issue.

"I'll Take That Seat When He Leaves!"

Another illusion stemming from a lack of appreciation of randomness involves the belief that if you're "running bad" it can be worth changing seats in the hope that that will change the quality of cards you're getting. The same notion may take the form of believing that if a player who has had a big win leaves the game, it is worth taking his seat in the hope that the seat will continue to be dealt many winning hands. Similarly a player who has had a good streak may continue to sit in the same seat everyday, harboring the assumption that the seat is "lucky" for him. The notion that you can identify a "hot" seat is not much different from the idea of being *on* a rush. It is another idea which assumes an ability to predict the future better than chance.

Imagine a large field in which sit 100 poker tables, each with 10 seats. Now imagine that 1,000 people are recruited to sit in these seats. Each is given a coin to toss over and over. Each person's job is just to sit in his seat and flip his coin continuously, stopping only for necessary breaks. They are to continue with this task for eight hours a day, for two months. Lets say they average seven hours of tossing per day, and complete 30 tosses per minute. Over 62 days that's 781,200 tosses per person. Somehow you record the results of each person's tosses. Somewhere near the 40 day mark you happen to spot several seats containing tossers who have just had their coins come up heads over 75 times out of their last 100 tosses.

If you were now to try to pick some seats containing tossers who are going to toss a disproportionately high number of heads in their *next* 100 tosses, should you pick one of the ones you've spotted? If you understood the coin toss analogy I applied to rushes, then it should be clear to you that it doesn't matter what seat you pick. If you were to believe that the tossers you've spotted are the best picks, then you would once again have to believe that something has changed in their coins making them now more than 50 percent likely to come up heads on a given toss.

Notice once again that this coin toss fantasy is analogous to the cards being dealt to those 1,000 seats. Various sorts of streaks will occur at various seats. But it is not accurate to say that one of these streaks *is happening*, only that it *has happened* in the immediate past. In fact, the notion that you should switch to the seat of a player who has been winning because that seat may continue to get good cards is like saying that you can take over another player's rush by replacing him in the same seat. The rush notion is fallacious to begin with, and so is this one. Again, however, this is not to say that there could be no valid reason for such a seat change. If you contend that you should move to a seat because of how other players are perceiving that seat, because they are intimidated by it perhaps, you at least have a certain logic to your argument. I don't happen to think it's an idea with much weight, but it is not the same thing as the "hot seat" notion.

"I Won't Play While He's Dealing!"

As you might have guessed by now the idea that certain dealers deal you more (or fewer) winning hands than others is just another variation on the same theme. This time picture a field containing 1,000 dealers. But instead of dealing cards each is flipping a coin. Again each flips his coin continuously for a long time. Now suppose that you stand in front of each dealer for 100 tosses. That's 1,000 dealers for 100 tosses each. During your times in front of these coin tossing dealers you note in each instance the number of times out of 100 that the coin comes up heads. Now it takes no knowledge of statistics, only common sense, to realize that out of the 1,000 dealers a few will toss a disproportionate number of heads, and a few will toss a disproportionate number of tails. Some will toss over, say, 65 heads, while some toss that many tails. But would you be willing to lay odds that one of those who tossed lots of heads is going to toss another head on his next toss? This is just a person tossing a coin! You should be able to see that the next toss has the same 50 percent chance as always of being a head.

It is the same with cards dealt. You sit through a large number of half hour stretches with various dealers and, *once you look back* on these stretches, some dealers will have *had* to deal you a disproportionate number of winners, others a disproportionate number of losers. So if you are not willing to lay odds on the coin toss, you should harbor no expectation that certain dealers are going to deal you more, or fewer, winning hands.

Energy Wasted on Illusions

For some readers the points made in this essay will have been ridiculously obvious. Others, however, will *still* maintain that they can tell when they're *on* a rush, or which seat is *currently* "hot," or which dealers they must avoid. In all honesty, as a serious poker player, I hope that a great many players continue to focus on these illusions. For by doing so they invest their energy in useless, sometimes costly pursuits rather than in what really matters at the poker table: The quality of their play. This is one of the many elements which keep the games beatable for players who invest their energy more wisely.

Bad Beat? Think Again.

One of the distinguishing characteristics of an advanced poker player is the ability to process multiple pieces of information simultaneously during a hand. For example, say a player believes he has a hand that is worth betting on the flop. Before acting he may be engaged in reading his opponents' hands while he determines the chances of his own hand improving, and considers the relative merits of betting out versus check-raising. Beyond this simple example, innumerable combinations of other variables vie for a player's attention on a routine basis. The best players are generally cognizant of and actively assessing more variables than other players. Yet even a skilled player sometimes misses an important piece of information. The most immediate consequence can be a misplayed hand. But failing to process all important variables in a hand can have less obvious consequences. One of the most common is that the missed information causes a player to assess an opponent's play incorrectly, costing him money in future hands played against that person.

I observed a hand recently in which this was the case. Before the flop, Ben, a weak, loose player, called in an early position. He was raised by Carl, in an early-middle position, a better than average, but not expert player who often tries to isolate weaker players with raises. The next player folded. Now Dean, a somewhat skilled and aggressive but far too loose player, made it three bets in a late-middle position. The players behind him folded. Ann, a poor player who will call raises preflop with weak hands, called in the big blind. Ben and Carl called. The flop came:

Everyone checked to Dean who bet. Ann, the big blind, raised. Ben folded, and Carl, the original raiser, made it three bets. Dean responded by capping it at four bets. The two players called. The turn was the:

Ann checked, but Carl bet out. Dean now raised again. Ann folded, and Carl called. The river was the five of clubs, and both players checked. Carl turned over:

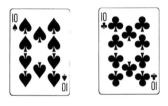

Dean won with:

Carl expressed anger and disgust at what he viewed as a bad beat. He included a sarcastic comment about Dean being psychic and knowing what was coming on the turn.

As I mentioned, Carl is a reasonably good, experienced player. He should know a bad beat when he sees one. (Whether bad beats are ever really bad, is another story.) Was there really anything bad about this beat? I don't think so. In fact, I think Dean played the hand quite well. Obviously Carl's primary criticism was of Dean's reraise on the flop. Yet, as I consider the situation I have to conclude that the reraise was almost mandatory. By putting in that extra bet Dean pressured Ann, in the big blind, to fold — something which would significantly increase his chances of winning the pot if he missed his flush, but paired either of his cards (and if she didn't fold he was now getting 2-to-1 odds on a hand that was probably less than 2-to-1 to win). While the extra raise did not have the desired effect on the flop, it was a reasonable choice especially given the relatively large pot. Whether or not Dean thought about it in this way, however, I don't know. He may simply have felt like playing his big flush draw aggressively. Still, the action itself was consistent with good play. Moreover, Dean's raise on the turn was again correct for a similar reason. If Ann held something like

getting her out, even at the risk of being reraised by Carl, prevented her from drawing out and taking the pot away from Dean in the event that his pair of jacks was in fact good. Even if Ann had called, at that point her odds would have been cut to the point where, depending on her hand, her call would probably have been incorrect. (See Sklansky's *The Theory of Poker* for the definitive discussion of these kinds of raises.)

My guess is that Carl failed to notice Dean's flush draw. Since he apparently was not considering a flush draw for Dean during the hand, when he saw the hands at the showdown, he saw only the ace and jack. He therefore figured Dean had played wildly and got lucky. It is hard to believe he would have been so critical had he been aware of the additional outs provided by the flush draw. By failing to process this aspect of the hand his understanding of Dean's playing style was slightly distorted. If he later assumes Dean to be a wilder player than he actually is, he may play incorrectly against him.

Once in a while I find myself in Dean's place, accused of putting a bad beat on someone when I was drawing to outs of which the accuser simply wasn't aware. I believe the cause of this sort of mental lapse is often emotional, as it appeared to be for Carl. For him, anxiety (or perhaps anger?) during the hand interfered with his cognition, preventing him from taking in all relevant information. Then his anger and disappointment at losing the pot again blinded him to the flush draw which lay before him on the table. (Incidentally, though debatable, his failure to bet out on the flop with his vulnerable pair of tens, hoping to be raised by Dean, thereby possibly knocking out Ann and Ben, is far more easily criticized than anything in Dean's play.)

There is no player who is aware of all relevant information at all times while he plays. But if emotion is interfering with your awareness while you play, you might need to consider the nature and causes of the reactions you are having. That is, *what* are you feeling (anxiety... anger... humiliation...?), and *why*. Though the answer to the latter question may ultimately be quite complex, anything you can discern may prove a useful first step toward reducing the problem. (Other essays that may offer some useful ideas in this area are those on the phenomenon of "tilt" and "A Poker Player in Therapy.")

Why Learn to
Beat Tougher Games?

Some poker players develop an erroneous idea concerning how to make substantial money at poker. Their idea, probably formed in the process of learning to beat small limit games, actually springs from one more valid — that of game selection. It is certainly true that the more game selective you are the better your hourly rate should be because you will spend more of your time in easier games. In the smaller games, where the competition is weak and games to chose from are plentiful, just a bit of game selection can usually have you playing in some of the easiest, "softest" games there are. Perhaps because this is what they've so often experienced in these games, the players I refer to arrive at the notion that an understanding of how most effectively to beat soft, loose games (which does require some specialized strategy) is all they really need to make plenty of money at poker. They decide, in fact, that learning how to beat tougher games is a waste of time.

One place where I've seen this idea expressed is in answer to questions posted on the Internet. A poster may ask, for example, how he should have played a particular hand. Let's say it was a hand which involved a preflop raise, then immediately became heads-up against the big blind. Sometimes such a question receives a response such as, "Well, your first mistake was playing in such a tight game to begin with."

While this attitude makes some sense in the lower limits, it can lead you astray if you hope to make the more substantial money that poker has to offer. To do that you will have to play in and beat middle to higher limit games. It can't be done in small limit games because, in any game, the betting limit sets a cap on what you can make over time. *And as you move up the limits, the games get tougher.* Furthermore, the higher you go, the fewer the opportunities for game selection.

If you want to make $40 per hour you will probably have to play at least $15-$30, and more likely somewhere between $20-$40 or $30-$60, depending on how well you play, where you play, and how much opportunity you have for game selection. At these limits you will frequently find yourself in games that are nothing at all like the soft small limit games. They are definitely beatable, but they would be considered quite tough if measured on the same scale used to judge the smaller games. (Exceptions do occur, and you should of course be ready to take advantage of unusually good games.) What if you want to make considerably more, say, over $100 per hour? Well then, get ready to play a minimum of about $60-$120, and be prepared to face some opposition that's tough by anyone's standards. Though such games do become softer at times, if you opt to play in them only when they resemble easy low limit games, you'll mostly be waiting around.

In my area, you don't even have to go very high to run out of game selection opportunities. Here, game selection possibilities are limited even at the $9-$18 level, nonexistent at $40-$80. If you want to make money in the one $40-$80 game here, then you have to be able to beat a game that often contains five or six of the best players in a metropolitan area of about 2.8 million people, and a couple more who are no slouches either. The same phenomenon occurs in areas where the highest limit game to be spread is smaller still. You may find that in a cardroom where the $15-$30 game is the biggest game in town, that game is at least semi-tough — especially if that form of poker is not new to the area.

This is not to discount the game selection opportunities that *are* available in middle and higher limit games. Especially if you are competent in more than one form of poker, and are located in one of the major poker centers, you will have some choices. Indeed, when you do have an unusual amount of choice (such as in Los Angeles or Las Vegas) proper game selection can make a very large difference in what you earn. That does not mean that the games you choose, the better games, will always (or even often) qualify as soft. Furthermore, even in the largest cardrooms, as you move up through the middle limits toward the higher limit games, your choices will inevitably thin out.

Clearly then, it pays to learn to beat tougher games. Of course when I say "tougher" I'm not referring to the very toughest games. Beating those games requires near world class skills, and even then may not be worth the bother. I'm talking about games, common at the middle limits, tending toward the tough side, but still quite profitable for many skilled players. These are the games you must learn to beat if you want to make decent money at poker. If you want to make quite a *lot* of money you'll have to learn to beat still tougher, higher limit games.

There is no secret to how you do this. You study the game while you get the playing experience. So learn how to beat the soft games, but also study the concepts which apply to tougher games. This will force you to think more deeply about poker, but will be well worth it. Do be game selective, but as you learn and improve don't always opt out of games with slightly tougher lineups; for they may be easier than what you'll be facing when you move up, and are good preparation for that move. As you become able to beat them for a fair hourly rate, enabling you to move up in the limits, your wallet will thank you.

Practicing Game Preservation

As poker players we strive to maximize our earn at the game. We develop and refine a diverse array of skills, striving to win perhaps one big bet per hour. Accordingly, if someone were to approach you with an idea which could save you, say, one quarter of a big bet per hour, would you not listen with interest? Yet there is an obvious idea which can save you much more. Strangely, few serious players take much interest in it, but to ignore it can cost you your *entire* hourly rate.

Educated readers might guess that I am referring to game selection, for it is an idea to which similar comments could apply. But the idea I wish to address is even more fundamental. It is game *preservation.* By game preservation, I mean acting to insure that your regular game (or games) thrives and does not dissolve, with the players no longer coming to the same cardroom for the same game on a regular basis. After all, without a game to play in you will have no opportunity to earn *any* hourly rate. It is therefore to your benefit to consider well what factors account for a game's ongoing health or, on the other hand, its demise.

If you live in an area with as much poker as Los Angeles, and have no interest in games above about the $30-$60 level, you may have little need to worry about losing your game. There are always other games or casinos to chose from, and a constant stream of players to populate them. Anywhere else, however, the loss of a game above the small limits can be a real problem. Even Las Vegas is not immune. In about 1996 Binion's Horseshoe lost its $20-$40 hold 'em game, a game they had spread for years. Though Vegas has a couple of other options for $20-$40 players, this news gives one pause. It shows that even a well established game in a cardroom which should have no shortage of new and regular players, can die out. Moreover, when it comes to the higher limits, even Los Angeles is not immune to losing games.

In the San Diego area I have seen numerous middle limit games come and go. Some of these games were successfully spread in busy cardrooms for several years running. They appeared to be thriving. Then, sometimes gradually, sometimes suddenly, they died. For example, some years ago I took a break of about four months from poker. At the end of the break I returned to the cardroom which spread my regular game (then $10-$20 with a "kill" or sometimes $15-$30). This game had survived for several years. I was thus dismayed to learn that it had dissolved during my absence. Impacted by the marketing, comps, and the reduced drop (the method of collection used instead of a rake in San Diego) offered by a larger casino, this cardroom saw an important piece of its business simply disappear. This was especially disturbing as I had become accustomed to playing in this, one of the few nonsmoking cardrooms in California at that time. Now I was forced to return to the smoke in order to keep playing. Thankfully, the game was revived two months later at the $15-$30 level, later changed to $20-$40, and survives at the time of this writing.

Needless to say, even such a temporary loss of a game is bad for both players and the house. The players lose their game which, for some, threatens their livelihood. The house sustains damage to its income which is even worse than it appears. If the cardroom manages to revive the game, they may find that some former players are reluctant to return, having found other games, quit playing, or developed resentment that the game they had counted on simply evaporated. So the house may have to work with a thinly populated, sporadically active game, and a need to rebuild a shrunken player base.

One factor which may be involved in the loss of a game is the simple flow of money from the weaker players to the stronger players. If there are too few players, or the weaker players are under-financed, the game's health can suffer. This is largely out of the control of the players or the house, but there are a number of other phenomena which affect the health of a game over which those involved do have some control. Some are small things, others are more profound, but they all add up in contributing to the health or demise of a game. The dissolution of my game prompted me to examine some of these phenomena. The result is a list of suggestions for players and cardrooms interested in preserving their games:

1. **Follow Mason Malmuth's suggestions.** In his *Poker Essays* and *Poker Essays, Volume II*, Malmuth provides numerous ideas which speak to the topic of game preservation. To review, he explains the importance of playing quickly and refraining from such time consuming practices as asking for deck changes and new setups when there is nothing wrong with the cards. (Players may get bored or frustrated and leave a slow game.) He points out the negative effects of criticizing weak players, discussing strategy at the table, asking to see another player's hand, pulling angle plays, and making plays which may humiliate a weak player. Additionally, he warns against insisting on technicalities and complete buy-ins for weaker players who are not trying to take advantage of the rules. For more on these and other ideas relevant to game preservation I refer the reader directly to Malmuth's writings.

2. **Nurture a friendly atmosphere at the table.** This is an elaboration of the idea that it is destructive to a game to criticize, or be hostile toward weaker players. Some professional players make an effort to avoid such behavior, but a few erroneously believe it to be to their benefit to act in an opposite manner toward better players. They apparently believe that if they are cold or rude toward better players, they will benefit by driving them off, and so keeping the "live ones" all to themselves.

This notion contains two serious flaws. First, professional and other winning players account for a significant, and stable part of the player base that keeps a game going from week to week. To drive these players off (which should not be easy to do, as most pros have learned to tolerate a variety of unpleasant behaviors on the part of some of their opponents) would take the backbone out of a game and threaten its demise. If you are a professional player, you need to accept that playing with some other pros at the table is a small sacrifice you must make in exchange for *having* a regular game to play in. Second, being rude or unfriendly toward *any* player, be they weak or skilled, creates an atmosphere of hostility which is witnessed by all the players at the table. When a recreational player encounters this, do you think he is likely to want to stay in the game or come back frequently in the future? I think not.

On a related note, people tend to feel most at ease in a social environment that they perceive as amiable and welcoming. A game that is dead silent, with nothing but a feeling of cutthroat competition hanging in the air is not going to feel this way to a new or inexperienced player. Thus, my advice is to do your part to create a friendly, sociable atmosphere at the table. Play hard but be friendly to your opponents. Try to initiate a little interesting or humorous conversation. (But do not bother players when they are in a hand or push it to the point of annoying anyone who would rather play quietly.) If you are stuck, and feeling sullen or frustrated, it is better to say nothing than to speak angrily or sarcastically to another player. If you are not an outgoing person you can still be polite and can make an effort to be at least a little more social than you might typically be. Look at it as a part of your work.

Note that this is an ideal to strive for. Though I try to follow my own advice, I like to think and observe a good deal at the table. Consequently I spend a good deal of my time playing quietly. Still, whenever game preservation is a concern I try to do my part to maintain an atmosphere to which people would not be loathe to return.

I have focused here only on promoting friendly social interaction. You may further improve the health of your game by thinking of other ways to make it an enjoyable environment for the players.

3. **Consider the impact of stack size.** There is an argument in favor of keeping a large stack of chips in front of you. The idea is that this will encourage players to think you are a winner, and will intimidate them so that they don't take shots at you, or otherwise play as aggressively against you. I believe there is at least a bit of truth to this. I have actually heard people express the belief that players whom I knew played a very flawed game were big winners simply because they usually had big stacks of chips on the table. (Note that you will not form such misperceptions about your opponents once you develop sufficient knowledge of the game to assess their skill purely from observing their play. Without this knowledge, you are vulnerable to being influenced and frequently misled by extraneous information such as stack size. For more see the essay, "An Illusory Winner.")

    So if you want to minimize other players' awareness of your downswings, keep a big stack. It is another step to say that this will substantially affect how they play against you. But it may at times produce some of the benefits mentioned above.

    There may, however, be other effects of stack size which bear on the issue of game preservation. For instance, indications that you are a winning player (e.g., consistently keeping a large stack) may keep weaker players away. That is, if they are intimidated by you they may not want to play in your game. I see this frequently. An average player looks at a game with a seat open, considers the lineup, and passes on the game. I am not sure that his concern is always about having to play against winning players. In some instances such a player probably sees the game as too "tight," a quality which he may or may not correlate with winning players. Clearly though, some players do make this connection. Others realize, at least, that in a zero-sum game there must be losers if there are to be winners. So if they see you as a winner, they have to conclude that you do not do much for their chances in that game. Thus, to the degree that you are seen by others as a winner, you are projecting a quality which does not attract them to your game.

This line of thinking leads to the conclusion that when you are concerned about game preservation, a small stack (which you can keep, by starting smaller and "coloring up") might actually be better for your image than a large stack. The small stack may make others less likely to see you as a winner, thus making your game more attractive to them. This is certainly preferable to being seen as a winner, but having no game in which to play.

There is another side to this argument. Some contend that there are players who are *attracted* to a game where they see large stacks. This is because they see what they believe to be an opportunity to take a small stack of their own up against some large stacks and perhaps win a lot of money. Of course, they fail to realize that a small stack in front of a good player is often like the tip of an iceberg. The professional's bankroll provides plenty of additional money that he can and will convert into chips should a downswing within a given session necessitate it. Players less educated in poker tend not to think about or even be aware of this. They look only at current stack size, figuring that's what is available for them to win in the present game.

Thus, we have one argument which holds that a small stack is conducive to game preservation, and another which advocates a large stack for the same purpose. I believe that each has validity. Some players are affected one way, others another, by variations in stack size. The trick, then, would be to identify how *specific* players are likely to be influenced by variations in *your* stack size. You must consider, among other things, your image with various players, what they know about you, how long they have played with you, and how sophisticated they are in their thinking about the game. You will then be in a position to decide what sort of stack to maintain.

That said, I don't believe that any of these effects of stack size is very strong. If you ignored them completely, it probably wouldn't matter very much. (I included this topic just to be thorough. I will admit that I usually just keep a stack size that is big enough to provide some reasonable insurance against the minor inconvenience of having to buy more chips.) Still, if you want to do all you can to keep your regular game alive you should probably think about them.

4.   **Be willing to play short-handed.** Unlike stack size, this is an *extremely* important factor in game preservation. One of the worst things for the long term health of a game is its breaking up frequently during the hours when players expect it to be spread. Typical players dislike this tremendously because they don't want to quit when they're stuck, without having had a chance to try to get even. When a game does too often break up this way, players soon learn that they cannot rely on the game to continue through the day (or night, as the case may be). They learn as well that it may or may not be there if they go to the cardroom during its normal hours. Encountering unreliability of this sort will eventually cause players to look elsewhere for a game they can count on.

What causes games to break? It usually happens when they become short-handed, and there is no list of players waiting. Typically, some or all of the players do not want to play short handed. They leave and the game breaks. (It is interesting to observe how this process often happens in stages. Perhaps some players quit and a nine-handed game becomes six-handed. Then a player who insists on a full game gets up and takes a walk waiting for the game to fill up again. Now someone decides that five handed is uncomfortable and decides to quit. Finally, at four handed, two more players decide they've reached their limit and quit as well. That leaves two players who, for one reason or another, don't want to play each other, so the game evaporates.)

As a serious player you can help prevent this. Simply be willing to play short-handed! If two or three players are willing to play short-handed, their game continues, and frequently fills up again as additional players arrive. In fact, of the many times I have sat in a short-handed game that did not break, there have been *very* few which did not fill up again within a couple of hours. (Of course I cannot speak about what happens in casinos I do not frequent. Furthermore, I have been mostly a day shift player. A game may be less likely to fill up late at night.)

If you are not skilled in short-handed play, then you would do yourself a favor by learning this facet of the game. (See my essay on short-handed play.) I am not suggesting that you should force yourself to sit and play heads-up against some very tough short-handed player. That is generally not necessary when typical games become short-handed. After all, even one relatively unskilled player can make a short-handed game quite playable if you are reasonably competent in this area of play.

Keeping a game together by playing short-handed is one of the most powerful tools for game preservation that you have at your disposal. It can literally save a game. Be willing, as well, to help start games by playing short-handed until they fill up. You will have no game to play in until someone starts it. Furthermore, you will find that often a game fills quickly once other players see that *they* do not have to play short-handed to start it.

Incidentally, feeling comfortable with short-handed play carries other benefits too. It gives you more playing time, adds variety to your poker experience, and is one of the more lucrative areas of poker play.

5. **Support game structures which are good for the survival of the game.** Mason Malmuth has written extensively on the

effects of various betting structures, and on the balance of luck and skill in poker. He has pointed out that the standard two level betting structure currently used in most limit poker games, with the small blind half the size of the big blind, seems to provide a near optimum balance of luck and skill. That is, an expert player can achieve a satisfactory hourly rate, but players experience fluctuations with a large enough standard deviation that weaker players will win often enough to stay interested in the game. On the other hand, there are some structures which unduly punish weaker players. No limit, pot limit, and spread limit games, for instance, provide the stronger player with an inordinate advantage. The result is that weaker players lose their money too quickly and consistently to allow (typically) for the long term survival of such games.

I have had experience with other structures which may threaten the survival of a game. One of these is the "kill" games played in many areas including parts of California. The usual procedure in one version of these games is as follows: Say you are playing a $10-$20 kill game. It is played as a normal $10-$20 game, except that if someone wins two pots in a row he has to "kill" it by posting a $20 blind, twice the normal big blind. The usual $5 and $10 blinds are posted by the appropriate players as well. Then, on that hand, the limit doubles to $20-$40. The same player keeps killing it until he loses a pot. Then the limit reverts to $10-$20. While many players enjoy the added bit of excitement this adds to the game, few realize that the kill structure gives an extra edge to better players. This is in large part because it is most often weaker players who are doing the "killing." They are more likely to win two pots in a row because they are in more pots, and stay to the end more frequently. Consequently, in a kill game they post more blinds than do the stronger players. This amounts to an extra monetary contribution made by already losing players. Add to this a few adjustments that a better player makes in his play in response to the kill structure, but a less educated player fails to make, and you have a significant increase in the advantage of the former over the latter.

The ratio of skill to luck is thus thrown out of balance in a kill game. Though this problem is far less pronounced than in a structure like no-limit, it is nonetheless bad for the survival of a game. If the health of a game is at all tenuous already, the use of such a structure could be enough to tip the scale toward the game's demise.

There is a variation on the kill structure that used to be seen sometimes in a cardroom that I frequented. We called it "leave it in." It is played as a kill game in which every pot is killed. In $10-$20 kill-"leave it in," there are the usual $5 and $10 blinds plus a $20 kill blind posted by the winner of every pot. Every hand is played at the $20-$40 limit. Notice that when you post the kill blind you are, in effect, just leaving in front of you the same blind (hence, "leave it in") that was posted by the winner of the previous pot. It simply travels from pot winner to pot winner, never going into anyone's stack. Therefore that blind does not contribute what a normal blind would to the value of the pot you are trying to win. You can never take possession of it as your own money because you must post it as soon as you win it. Its value is that it gains you free entry to the next pot, barring a raise before the action gets to you. Moreover, because you never really take possession of it, it costs you nothing to post the kill blind; you just leave it in.

What this game therefore amounts to is a $20-$40 game with $5 and $10 blinds. This small blind structure allows for, and in some respects *dictates* extremely tight play. Less educated players, who do not understand this are going to lose even more consistently than usual. They are at a greater disadvantage here than in the regular kill structure. Obviously the "leave it in" structure may seriously damage a game's chances for survival over the long term. (For a description of a similar, but even more unbalanced structure see Malmuth's discussion of "The Rock Game" in *Poker Essays, Volume II.*)

Numerous other structures have been tried for hold 'em. But the undeniable fact is that for a game to survive, it must attract both skilled regulars and casual recreational players. This requires a structure which correctly balances skill and luck. Today's standard structure comes close to producing that balance. It is to your benefit as a serious player to support this or a similar structure for hold 'em.

6. **Educate management on the impact of a high rake, time charge, or drop.** Consider a game with a two dollar "drop" (the way players are charged to play in some games in California). What is the impact of raising the drop to three dollars? In a fast moving game this one dollar increase can mean between 10,000 and 20,000 extra dollars per month taken from the players. (The higher figure applying to games which run for, say, twenty hours per day.) This has the same effect as adding an additional player who beats the game for ten to twenty thousand per month. The impact of such a move on a middle limit game should be obvious. If a game has any trouble surviving because of under-funded, losing players, it will now be pushed beyond the breaking point.

7. **Develop a mutually beneficial relationship with cardroom management.** Through their publicity, promotions, treatment of customers, professionalism, spreading the right games, and so on, cardroom management has more influence than any player over the establishment and preservation of games. It is crucial, therefore, for the professional or other serious player to communicate with management.

If you see something which may undermine the health of your game, let them know. Offer opinions or suggestions if you have thought them through and believe they are in the best interest of the game. At the same time, offer to do what you can as a player to nurture the game. Of course much of what you can do is listed above, but management might additionally suggest something simple such as arriving earlier to help start the game each day.

I hope I have impressed upon you that game preservation is of paramount importance to the serious player. Without a game you may be faced with difficult decisions concerning your livelihood or place of residence. It is far easier to do your part to preserve the game you already have. By following the suggestions provided, you may be able to keep your game alive and healthy.

Short-Handed
Play: Don't Miss Out

A majority of poker players shy away from short-handed games. That's too bad. They miss out on some of the most stimulating and *profitable* poker there is. Short-handed play calls for more mix in your play, more deception, and often more psychology than ring game play. What's more, you get to play a lot more hands! In all these ways, short-handed play has more of what many of us feel poker is all about.[13]

More Profit Short-Handed?

I have just suggested that short-handed play can be more profitable than play in a full game. If you are in doubt, consider this: A typical ring game may contain a couple of very good players, a couple of fair players, two or three mediocre players, and a couple of really bad players. Clearly, you can profit more from the bad players than from the others. In fact, many experts believe that the bulk of your profit in such games comes from the really bad and, to a lesser extent, the mediocre players.

So wouldn't you do better if the fair and very good players were not even in the game? If you could take everyone else out and just play against the two really bad players, wouldn't that be best of all? It would truly maximize your opportunities to make better decisions than your opponents. You can have this utopian poker situation — or close to it — when you play short-handed. Of course, you have to be a bit game selective. But in my

---

[13] That said, I would *not* argue that short handed play is necessarily more complex, or requires much more skill than play in a full game. But it does highlight *different* skills.

experience, when games get short-handed, one or two bad or mediocre players frequently stay to play, and that's all you need. If you are lucky you will be left with only a couple of bad players. Sometimes, however, another good player will stay as well. Still, the ratio of bad to good players can make this a good situation for you.

Bear in mind as well that lots of decent ring game players do not play so well short-handed. Also, some losing, loose, aggressive, ring game players do much better in a short-handed setting. Naturally, you factor in these points when assessing who is a "good" player in a short-handed game. Nevertheless, it may take only one weak short-handed player to make the situation worthwhile. On a number of occasions I have played three-handed with one of the best short-handed players I know. Obviously, the profit comes not from the tough player, but from the bad player who has opted to play in this game. Note that here I was in a game in which half of the other players played poorly.

Another factor adding to your profit potential in short-handed games is the number of hands played per hour. Though the pots are smaller, in a short-handed game you play *many* more hands per hour than in a full game. More hands played means more profit. Even in a ring game in which you are surrounded only by bad players, you do not have anything like this. In fact, in such a game you will frequently be sitting out hands, watching bad players trade their money around. Compare that to playing heads-up against a weak player. There you will have one opportunity after another to outplay and profit against a player whose decisions are worse than yours. (Note, however, the caution below about heads-up play.)

So when your game becomes short-handed, look at who is left. If you have been quitting when the game is actually rich in weak players, you've been making a bad play.

Short-Handed Play
and Game Preservation

For the serious middle or higher limit player there is an additional, extremely important reason to play short handed. If your cardroom is not in one of the major poker centers, then your game may well be surviving tenuously — here today, breaking up midday tomorrow, maybe not being spread at all during some periods. I submit that *a major factor contributing to a game being spread inconsistently in a given cardroom, is players' unwillingness to play short-handed.*

If you ever want to feel like a cardroom hero, keep playing when your game gets down to five-handed or less. If some of your opponents hang in there as well, chances are strong that the game will fill up again within a couple of hours. Then you will have a sense of what your staying to play accomplished. I have seen it happen perhaps 80 percent of the many times I have been involved in this scenario myself. A game that might have evaporated and not reformed until the next day, continued on instead. This does wonders for the overall survival of your game. It reduces the frequency of players calling or, worse yet, coming to the cardroom only to be told there's no game. Obviously, when they too often hear that there is no game, some players are going to give up on the cardroom.

Be Prepared for Some Fluctuations

Short-handed play does tend to magnify your fluctuations. Playing hands with small edges aggressively to the river creates unavoidable swings. You should be ready for this. The swings are partially tamed, however, by the greater overall edge you can have short-handed if you are a bit game selective, and by the larger number of hands played over a given time. As you improve in your short-handed play, your swings should decrease as long as you remain selective of your opponents. In fact, in my experience players' fears of the fluctuations are often exaggerated. Yes, they are greater, but if you play against the right opponents they can be smaller than you might guess. When your edge is very pronounced you may be surprised at how modest they are.

Short-Handed Tips

Here's a few tips to help with your short-handed game. They should be especially helpful to those of you who normally avoid playing once several players have left the game.

1. **Adapt what you've learned in this ring game situation.** One of the simplest ways to keep your thinking on the right track when playing short-handed is to keep in mind a basic point made by Sklansky and Malmuth in the older editions of their *Hold 'em Poker for Advanced Players*: When you are playing short-handed it is much like playing in a blind or in late position in a full game after most of the other players have folded. If you know how to play your hand on the button, after everyone has folded to you, then you are probably close to knowing how to play it when you are on the button in a four-handed game.

2. **Note that your opponents' attitudes change.** Add to the above an awareness that the "psychology" of the game changes when short-handed, and you begin to have a more thorough understanding of short-handed play. As Malmuth points out in *Poker Essays*, players in a short-handed game are expecting you to raise with weaker hands, and so will defend their blinds more tenaciously. A hand, therefore, like

with which you might routinely try stealing some players' blinds in a full game, might need to be folded (or might be worth just a call) a little more often when playing short-handed. Focus more on hands with some high card value.

You will find that when the game gets very short handed, some of your opponents start showing down some pretty scraggly hands. Don't be surprised to encounter hands like

or

This is part of the changed mind set in short-handed games. Many players have only half a notion of short-handed play and believe that they have to start playing very "loosely," perhaps playing anything with a tiny bit of high card value. They therefore play many more hands than they would in the analogous full game situation mentioned above in tip number one. Be aware that this is their thinking so that you will know what's happening if you find that even in a three or four handed game you are playing more tightly than your opponents.

3. **Stay aware of how your opponents are perceiving you.** While this is important in a full game as well, it becomes

crucial when playing short-handed against the same players for any length of time. These players are playing a great many hands against *you* and are often far more tuned in to how you are playing than they would be in a full game.

Thus, for example, even more than usual, if you've just been caught bluffing a couple of times, you may need to sit back and wait a bit until you have some sort of real hand, before pushing it again. Still, you certainly don't need a monster. But you'd better have some sort of pair, and be prepared to get played with by an opponent who may think you are stealing yet again. Likewise, if you do make a big hand in this spot, be less inclined to slowplay it, as you will likely get more than full value for it from your suspicious opponents. On the other hand, if you've shown down nothing but high cards for a while it might be a good time to come in for a raise with that 7♠5♠ or other similar hand. (Note that short-handed something like

may qualify as high cards.) Such a hand should now have better implied odds for you, as your opponents are less likely to put you on it if you hit something.

4. **Use more deception.** Because the pots are smaller and usually heads-up, you can afford to put a little more deception in your game. For instance, you might slowplay a set (or even as little as top pair) on the flop, that you would raise with in a multiway pot, so as to make it expensive for drawing hands. In the short-handed setting, it is less likely that the draw is there against you, and letting your opponent

catch up a bit or perceive you as weaker than you are may well be worth the increased risk.

5.   **Play aggressively and semi-bluff frequently.** Do this against most opponents; but don't forget who you are up against. If your opponent is a calling station, then just as in a full game, you must semi-bluff less often, and use less deception.

6.   **Balance your aggressive play with some passive calling as well.** As your opponents will usually be playing aggressively, let them hang themselves sometimes by checking and calling with a hand like one pair, much as you would against a habitual bluffer.

7.   **Be aware that heads-up play is unique.** It is a mistake simply to equate heads-up play with, three or four-handed play. The drop from three down to only two players is significant. While your skills from general short-handed play help in playing heads-up, the latter does have a unique character. In my experience the swings are noticeably greater as well. Give it thought and study, and get some solid experience before opting to play heads-up with anyone who is experienced and likely to be skilled in that arena of play.

8.   **Be sure to get a rake cut.** In a short handed game a normal rake (say, about $3 taken out of most pots) is too much. Depending on the limit, it may be insurmountable. Make sure the cardroom substantially reduces or eliminates the rake for you as long as the game is short-handed. After all, you are holding the game together for them until more players come along. They should be happy to give you this break.

I hope I have convinced you that you should often stay to play when your game gets short-handed. Perhaps the tips I have provided will help reticent players feel more comfortable pursuing this very lucrative area of play. Learn about playing short-handed, and look for opportunities to get inexpensive experience, or to play against opponents who will not be too challenging. For an excellent and much more thorough treatment of the topic of short-handed play, on both the theoretical and practical levels, see *Hold 'em Poker for Advanced Players: 21ˢᵗ Century Edition.*

How I Learned Poker: Part I

No university offers poker as a major. You will not find a neatly organized curriculum or specific syllabi to follow. The serious student of the game is left to structure his learning in whatever way he pleases. This happens to be one of the things I have always loved about poker. Either studying or playing, you are on your own, free to make decisions and to act on them, with no one to answer to but yourself. On the other hand, this lack of any standard learning method can make the process of acquiring poker skills a frustrating one. Though I will not attempt here to provide such a method, I will share some of the steps I took and resources I used to learn this complex game. I will focus mostly on those tools I found valuable. That is not to say there were no counterproductive efforts, or other missteps along the way.

Here in Part I, I will cover much of the foundation of my poker education. I will focus in Part II on subsequent phases and more "advanced" aspects of my poker learning process. I hope you will find ideas that will help in your own journey toward understanding this fascinating game.

A Fateful Trip

I began playing poker in the summer of 1987. A weekend trip to Las Vegas piqued my curiosity about poker and blackjack. But since I was attracted to competitive strategy, poker quickly took over as the game that held my interest. I was a graduate student at the time, working on a Ph.D. in clinical psychology. It was only natural, therefore, that I took a student's approach to learning poker. That meant looking for books to study. Disappointed by the poker books then available in standard bookstores, I ordered Doyle Brunson's *Super/System: A Course in Power Poker* after seeing it mentioned in a magazine article. I then decided that I might find other good poker books by looking for works by

Brunson's collaborators. These books marked my introduction to the serious poker literature. I believe the first good poker books I read were *Super/System* and Sklansky's *Winning Poker* (now *The Theory of Poker*), and *Hold 'em Poker*. For someone who had barely played a hand of poker, this was a slightly overwhelming introduction to the game. I was still hazy on the basic rules and procedures of the game as I struggled to absorb the intricacies of the semi-bluff and the strategic differences between limit and no-limit poker. Today, however, a player just starting out can work his way up, beginning with good quality introductory texts such as the *Fundamentals of Poker* by Malmuth and Loomis.

As a result of my experience, I recommend that anyone just learning poker first seek the help of someone with some experience to guide him through the basic routine of play. When you know *nothing whatsoever* of the game, it's hard to learn from books. The first time I gathered some friends together (who knew as little as I did) to try playing for nickels and dimes, I referred constantly to a weak poker book I'd found at a local bookstore, checking on rules and procedures as we progressed. The book's instructions were confusing and we interpreted its discussion of structured limit betting to mean that if we were playing, say, 5¢-10¢ limit, we could bet any amount on a 5¢ betting round as long as it was in multiples of 5¢! In other words, we played a funny little form of no-limit poker. Eventually, of course, we straightened things out.

Into the Cardrooms

My first venture into a public cardroom came after maybe ten hours of this fumbling home poker. I had thought high draw would be a good form of poker to start with since to me it was the classic game that came to mind when I thought of poker. So I had gone about memorizing what I could of Mike Caro's high draw chapter in *Super/System*. I managed to commit to memory a good portion of the advice on play before the draw, then figured I needed to start getting a little playing experience to bring to life what I was reading. So one Sunday I headed North from San Diego to Los Angeles, where I found the suburb of Gardena and the Normandie Casino. There I found my way to a $2-$4 jacks-or-better draw game. I managed to lose only $19 in three hours. I also managed to draw some scorn for standing pat with nothing and betting out after the draw to win the pot, only to be asked to show my mandatory jacks or better "openers." I apologized as the action was rewound and the players returned their money. I was taken aback, however, by the level of irritation shown by the other players in response to my simple beginner's mistake. These players, I was beginning to see, took their game rather seriously. Before leaving the Normandie, I got into a conversation with a friendly local who informed me that Texas hold 'em was really the hot new game in town.

A few weeks later I discovered the poker in San Diego County. Initially, I found one of the Indian reservation casinos. I went there one night with a friend who also thought he might like to learn the game. After observing some hold 'em and seven-card stud eight-or-better games, we bought into a little hold'em tournament for $5. Neither of us lasted very long, but in talking afterward we decided that hold 'em had to be the game to learn. I must say that even as poker "infants" that night our reasoning was a bit like that of seasoned professional players. We concluded that in addition to being popular, hold 'em appeared to be a complex game. Its complexity, we figured, would serve us well in the long run. As graduate students (he in electrical engineering) we were, I must admit, a bit arrogant about our intellectual abilities relative to what we assumed were those of the average poker player. We knew we would be able to develop a thorough understanding of this difficult game, and so have a big edge over those who we figured surely wouldn't study it in the same depth.[14]

---

[14] I now believe we were partially right. Our background in fields requiring logical thinking and familiarity with studying new and complex topics did give us a certain edge. Moreover, my willingness to devote considerable time to the project gave me a

Keeping Tuition Affordable

My friend did not continue much further with poker, but I remained fascinated and began to study hold 'em. I've never been a "gambler" in the popular sense of the word. It was not the element of gambling that attracted me to poker. Instead, I found gratification in learning, then successfully applying strategy. Had I been able to take the gamble out of the game, I would have, but during this early learning period, I knew I had to expect to lose some money until I knew the game well enough to beat it. The question was how to lose the minimum until I had acquired the requisite knowledge and skill. Today, a useful tool in this regard is the poker playing software available for the personal computer. It allows you to play countless hands against simulated players and acquire at least an initial feel for the game before risking money. (At the time of this writing it still has clear limitations, but is certainly valuable for that purpose.) In 1987, however, I was working without such software. I recall using some primitive poker software a bit later, but it was of very limited use.

I settled on a two-pronged approach to keep tuition reasonable. First, I played in a number of very small buy-in tournaments. Some of the cardrooms had buy-ins ranging from free to about $10. Through these, I reasoned, I could pick up some experience while putting very little money at risk. I played in perhaps 15 of these. I actually turned a profit because one tournament was a weekly free entry event, and the winner received $100 in the form of a rack of chips. After attending a seminar in Las Vegas at which David Sklansky gave a couple of

---

serious advantage over anyone less committed. Our conclusion however, that hold 'em was the *only* game to learn was a bit narrow. Seven-card stud, for example, is similarly complex, and would have made a good choice for the same reasons. But since it was not spread in our area, we based our conclusions on what we saw.

key tournament tips, I applied them to this little weekly event, and won it several times out of maybe eight or nine tries. Undoubtedly I got lucky, but the competition was mostly very weak. These little tournaments did serve their purpose for me, but a player using cheap tournaments to acquire early experience should keep in mind the important differences between tournament and live game play.

The other part of my approach to learning cheaply was to ration my poker money over periods of time with playing sessions interspersed with reading and study of the game. That way I could keep playing with some regularity without worrying about losses. Losses served as motivators to study more, learn general poker theory, familiarize myself with the specifics of hold 'em, and analyze my own play.

My study materials at that time centered on the works then available by Sklansky, Malmuth, Caro, Brunson, and anything else I could find, such as columns in *Poker Player*, then the main poker periodical. For me it was rather slow going. The logic of poker did not come particularly easily to me, and I did not bring much natural "card sense" to the game. I had to struggle first to understand a piece of poker theory, and then to take the step of applying it in practice. The latter was made more difficult by the anxiety I experienced when I played in a cardroom. I typically felt quite nervous as I played. It was, I suppose, a kind of performance anxiety. After all, poker players must play hands in front of "spectators" — their opponents in the hand and the other players at the table. The anxiety of course interfered with the clarity and efficiency of my thinking. With much experience, however, I became accustomed to cardroom play and able to think calmly about the application of theory to the realities of the game around me.

In that early period I sought out the smallest hold 'em games I could find. It was only sensible, I figured, to play as small as possible until I knew I was beating the game. (Today the rakes in small games are often too high, and this approach may not be as advisable. Even then, I was fighting a sizable rake in proportion to the limit.) Three times I even took this to the extreme by flying to Las Vegas to play in the tiniest casino hold 'em game I had been able to locate, a $1-$2 game at the Four Queens. (To me it somehow spoiled the whole idea to factor in silly things like airfare.) It was spread as a beginners' game. A dealer would explain the game to a group of first time players, let them practice a bit, then turn it into a live game. Having already developed an appreciation for the importance of game selection, I saw this as quite the "juicy" opportunity. Here I was, the "aspiring to aspire to be a pro" player sitting down among the neophytes who had no idea what a poker force they were dealing with. I lost $13 over those three sessions. Poker is hard.

Years later I learned that one of the best players I had come to know in San Diego had also made trips to that game in the early stages of his learning. I think we simply shared a sensible desire to take the risk out of the game to whatever extent we could while we learned.[15]

Going Beyond the Books

Because I was busy with school, my poker play was sporadic for the first couple of years, involving only about 60 hours of casino play spread over 22 sessions, mostly in $2-$4 games. I had spent more time studying the game than playing it. Once I finished my graduate work, I decided it was time to put in more hours at the tables and see how I fared. I played about 140 more hours over the next four months. Despite noticeable progress, my

---

[15] I should note, though, that ultimately one should not let such a desire get in the way of a willingness to make risky plays when they are warranted. In fact, that friend I mentioned now plays hold 'em in a style characterized in large part by a willingness to push very small edges. Though my own play pushes the limits a bit less, I too am quite willing to take risks with marginal edges when I believe the situation merits it.

results for those 200 hours of play suggested to me that I might not yet be playing at a winning level. It was not enough time to be at all certain, but my losses had outnumbered my wins, and my results in $2-$4 and $3-$6 games were still negative.

Not satisfied, I resolved to take my poker education beyond the books. While I knew I had not fully absorbed the concepts I had read about, I believed I could accelerate my education through private instruction. I had always learned best when I had the chance to ask a lot of questions. I did some checking and found that David Sklansky was available for private consultations. I knew his credentials were the best, but his time was not cheap. I worried that I might have to spend thousands of dollars over some extended period to see real results. In truth, I was prepared to do that. Having spent most of my life up to then in school, I saw it simply as the tuition I should expect. But when I contacted David, described my background, and asked how many hours of instruction it might take to see real benefits, I was surprised and pleased that he answered, "Maybe three." So I organized a list of my most pressing poker questions and problems and, by telephone, did my first hour with Sklansky.

Most of the consultation centered on two areas I had found particularly vexing: How to play in loose games and how to play against maniacs. David clarified things I had read, but also provided much that went beyond the books. This filled in the gaps in my understanding to the point that I was able after just that first hour to play with much more confidence in loose games and wild games.

In fact, it turned out David had overestimated in guessing it would take three hours to see results. The effect of just that first session on my poker cash flow was most impressive. Though I couldn't be positive because of a small sample size, from what I could see, my results changed immediately. My frequency of winning sessions went up dramatically and, with a couple more consultations along the way, I gradually earned back what I had lost — and continued winning. A graph would show an abrupt leveling out followed by a clear reversal of the losing trend I had experienced before that time.

Of course it wasn't quite that simple. Certainly there were fluctuations. They are a part of poker. In fact, I did have my share of disheartening losses, and suffered some setbacks when I tried to move up in limits. But in time I always overcame those. Overall, my results since that early period have been steady and positive.

In retrospect, initiating those consultations with Sklansky may have been the single most important step I ever took in structuring my learning process. I consulted with David off and on in subsequent years as I developed my play and worked my way into the middle limits. Through my own thinking about the game, I was able to magnify the gains of the consultations. Often something David would explain would lead me to new insights in other areas as I began to see conceptual connections and to gain the groundwork necessary to arrive at valid ideas on my own. Though I play successfully at higher limits now, I fully intend to consult further with David as I continue with poker. His depth of knowledge is unmatched. So like the golf pro going back to his teacher for a tune up, I will continue from time to time to hone my game with his "coaching."

How I Learned Poker: Part II

Having described in the previous essay much of my early learning and progression into winning play, I begin here with my transition out of the small limit games into the middle limits. This marked the clear beginning of a new phase in my poker education.

Moving Up

Another key element in my growth as a player resulted simply from moving up to the $10-$20 level. I had played $10-$20 several times in Los Angeles a few years earlier, and though I had netted only a small loss, I dropped back down to the small limits, uncomfortable with the swings I'd experienced. Subsequently, I made a stubborn commitment to move up only as my bankroll passed certain thresholds which I knew would allow for comfortable play at each new limit. Moreover, these were high thresholds, calculated with relation to hourly rates that were probably lower than what I could actually expect to achieve at each limit. I did not want to worry about losing my bankroll, and I insisted on building my bankroll solely through poker. If I had won my way into each new limit, I knew I would feel more confident at that limit. While this was true, I was probably ready to make the move up to $10-$20 well before I finally did. I would now suggest that newer players who have the financial resources to do so without winning their entire bankrolls, should experiment with moving up as soon as they are reasonably confident that their skills are sufficiently developed to win at the next level. Remember, you can always move back down. It is quite common for players fully capable of winning at higher limits to have to hop up and down a bit between limits for a while before fully settling at the next higher limit. Assuming you want to maximize your earnings, the advantage to moving up when you have the skills

106

and resources to do so, simply means you can earn more, allowing you to move up yet again that much sooner, and so on.

In my case, it took two potent confidence boosters to nudge me into stepping up to $10-$20 before I had reached the very high bankroll threshold I had set for myself. First, a player who had played at higher limits than I, and whose ability I had greatly admired, stunned me when he said in conversation, "I'd say there are about ten people in San Diego County who can play, and you're one of them." Before you have accumulated a great deal of experience, the short-term luck factor in poker can blur your vision in judging your ability relative to others. This single comment opened my eyes to the possibility that I had been underestimating my readiness to move up.

The second nudge came about a month later as I played in a $6-$12 game. A young traveling pro from Dallas was in the game that day waiting for the $10-$20 game to start. He asked if I played $10-$20. When I said I didn't, he offered to take forty percent of my action at $10-$20 so that I would effectively still be playing $6-$12. About an hour later, he again brought it up, saying, "I *definitely* want forty percent of *your* action." That this player, who appeared quite good, was eager to "invest" in my poker ability was enough to make me rethink the timing of my move up. Shortly thereafter I began playing $10-$20 regularly, did well, and from that day on have continued gradually to work my way up the limits.

Poker on a New Level

Once I did make the move up, I could tell that I was confronting a new, challenging level in my poker education. I played mostly in a small cardroom in a $10-$20 hold 'em game which was the biggest game they spread. (This game later evolved into $15-$30, then $20-$40.) Here, for the first time, I was faced with some professional, and similarly skilled, non-professional players on a daily basis. A core of players, tougher than any I had previously encountered, frequented the game, some of whom I still play with in bigger games today. That game also featured some maniacs, and semi-maniacs who, despite their style of play, were more effective thinkers and hand readers than I had had to deal with in the lower limits. This combination of tougher players and thinking maniacs made for a challenging adjustment. I believe for me it was an excellent poker "school." I should add that there were enough unthinking, generally bad players as well to make the game more than adequately profitable.

At this level, I was able to begin exploring more fully many of the tactics and levels of thinking I had studied in the poker literature. Semi-bluffs, for instance, must be kept to a very low frequency in many loose games. But here, I had not only the opportunity, but a need to become more conversant with them. In addition, with players now putting me on hands and thinking about what I put *them* on, I had to learn to apply the tool of *thinking about what my opponent was thinking* during play, a key ingredient to success above the small limits.

Also about that time, I first began to regularly encounter opponents whose play was similar in many respects to my own. This provided a sort of validation through observation. In the small limits it is easy when you are trying to play well but are not yet very experienced, to develop self doubt as you encounter so few others who play anything like the way you do. In addition, when you do see someone who plays as tightly as you do, for example, you have no evidence that this is an element which can help you succeed at progressively higher limits. On the other hand, seeing the same style at a higher limit, exhibited by a player who you know worked his way up and is succeeding at that level, supports your understanding that you are doing something right.

Taking this one step further, the better opponents against whom you play present you with an opportunity to learn by observing them. I watched closely what my more skilled opponents did, and worked to uncover the logic of plays they made that I did not immediately understand. When you play against better players, you will in time be exposed to all manner of sophisticated plays. Don't pass up the opportunity to think about what you see. Just be sure to apply analysis to distinguish between genuinely good play and poor play masquerading as good. Even most fairly good players exhibit plenty of the latter, as well as the former. Note that I am not advocating going out looking for tough games. Though an occasional foray into a known tough game may be instructive, you will generally be confronted by enough tough opponents as you navigate the middle limits without seeking out games that are full of them. Do be game selective.

Making Use of
More Tools and Resources

One tool I began to use more seriously than I had before was a "player book," a notebook in which I outlined details of opponents' play and constructed strategies for playing against them. By selecting an opponent who had given me trouble, dissecting his play against me, and determining how best to counter it, I deepened my understanding of poker while improving my results against that opponent. While my use of such a notebook is now more limited, I recommend it strongly to players adjusting to new limits or otherwise still on the steep part of the poker learning curve.

The growth of my understanding of poker during and after my move to the middle limits also owes much to discussion with other good players. It is not always easy to get winning players to share their knowledge. Many are fearful of divulging their "secrets." But, in my experience the gains from good discussion far outweigh any cost of sharing information. After all, even in a pure teacher-student relationship the teacher often gains as much as the student as he clarifies and organizes his own thinking.

In recent years a new dimension has been added to this dialogue. Sites for discussion of poker on the Internet have seen tremendous growth and often are home to sophisticated debate among players of all levels of knowledge. Now, for the first time in poker history, you might, for instance, see a veteran player, drawing on his years of experience, debate the pros and cons of betting versus check-raising in a particular situation with a young math major just starting out in poker, but with a sophisticated ability to attack the question with mathematical and logical analysis. I bought a new computer and got on line for the first time in the spring of '98 just so I could participate in these discussions on the Two Plus Two Forums at www.twoplustwo.com. This web site for the publishing company of the book you are reading has become well known for hosting the most substantive poker discussions on the net. Learning from others on these forums, and clarifying my thinking through the effort to explain ideas has since become a key way by which I keep sharp my ability to apply the thought processes of poker. The forums have grown so much that it is now nearly impossible to keep up with all the new information that appears. With the amazing growth and development of the Internet, there is no telling how this and other sites will evolve. Suffice it to say that players who are serious about deepening their understanding of poker are missing out if they fail to take advantage of all that is offered by these new Internet resources.

Sharpening "Feel"

In my view, the best poker player is the one who is strong in both his objective knowledge of the game and his *feel* for it. Though any thorough attempt to define "feel" would be worthy of its own essay, in essence I am talking about some combination of card sense and a sensitive attunement to the play of one's opponents. Some players either come to the game with or quickly develop a good feel for poker. They are "naturals." But I believe feel can be developed as well. Thus, another facet of my efforts to improve my poker has been to work, to the extent that I could, on this development. I have sharpened my feel for the game partly through the simple process of noting well those periods when I judged my play to be at its best, and working to identify as much as possible what was going on during those times, including elements of my sensory experience, in order to improve my chances of recreating those states in the future.

Feel is also simply a product of experience. The more you play, if you are also investing energy in trying to improve your game, the better your feel gets. A related point is that short-handed play puts a premium on feel. Therefore, getting a fair amount of short-handed experience will greatly improve some areas of your feel for poker, though not all that you gain there will transfer fully to some areas of ring game play. Sometimes I play short-handed not only for its profit potential (which is often greater than that of a ring game), but to make sure I stay in touch with the aspects of play which it highlights.

Learning From Losses

A look back on my time in poker suggests to me that a particular strength of mine as a player has been my persistence in using setbacks, such as periods of running badly, as opportunities for learning. Though I have long been well aware that it is statistically possible for a very good player to have unavoidable, frighteningly long losing (or breaking even) streaks purely as a result of the chance element in poker, I believe it is usually wise, when bad runs or individual big losses do occur, to assume first that poor play contributed significantly to the results. This is my natural tendency anyway, but I believe it has served me well. I have long been driven to scrutinize my play, thereby giving me the best chance to correct any problems, which may have damaged my results. Experience has taught me to do this at the first *hint* of any problem in my play. I recommend you do the same. (It is of course smart to examine your play *all* the time, but it is *crucial* when you've been losing.)

In other words, when you suffer a bad loss or any sort of losing streak, immediately take a hard look at how you've been playing. If you ignore for long what is happening, you may find yourself in a cycle from which it is difficult to escape. For example: You get a little sloppy in your play while at the same time running badly. You feel frustrated about your poor results. Your frustration affects your play, leading to further disappointing results, and on it goes. A bit of classical conditioning may occur as well, and the very act of playing poker becomes a stimulus for frustration and bad play. It may be difficult for most players to come to an appreciation of this without experiencing it. Still, I hope my cautions may save some money for readers who take them to heart. Consider using a setback as motivation for learning. You may not only return to your own previous best level of play, but may deepen your knowledge of poker, thereby reaching a *higher* level than before. (For more, see the essay, "Subtle Losses of Judgment.")

One method by which you can examine your play is to make a note during a session of any hand you feel you may have played badly. After the session, record the hand, nature of the error, its probable cause (e.g., acting too fast without careful hand reading, failing to anticipate action behind you, tilt, or what have you), and what you need to do to minimize the chance of making the same mistake in the future. I have used this method in addition to taking notes on hands I felt I played well. But you may find some other system more helpful. The key is to analyze where you may be erring, and correct the problem. By noting your good plays as well, you develop a record which may serve as a profitable reference for you in the future.

If I Had It To Do Over Again

What would I do differently if I were learning poker all over again? On a general level I would try to approach it in a more structured way. While I probably did impose more structure on my learning than do most players, I know that a very well thought out and organized sequence of study can greatly accelerate the learning of nearly any subject. Had I approached it a little differently, I believe I could have made my way up the limits faster. In fact, I submit that most veteran players would be surprised at how fast a reasonably bright student of the game can become quite successful with the right course of study combined with time at the tables.

Key to this more structured approach would be to seek expert advice sooner and more often. I believe if an ambitious beginner were to ask me for some general guidelines to think about as he embarked upon a journey of learning poker, I could provide several key ideas that would speed up his progress. Thus, were I just starting out again, I believe I would make that first phone call to Sklansky, looking for just such ideas, as soon as I'd read two or three key books and acquired just enough playing time (perhaps as little as 20 hours) to absorb an initial feel for one game. I would then continue with more frequent consultations, asking for help in identifying the gaps in my knowledge so that I could fill them in. One way to identify such gaps is to examine individual hands you have played. Your mistakes will point toward what you need to learn.

I hope this summary of some of the elements I have found helpful in learning poker will prove useful to those of you striving to become better players. Unless you bring exceptional talent to the game, you will find that learning to play poker well takes a good deal of time. Fortunately, the resources for learning are growing rapidly. The poker literature is far more extensive today than when I started out, and the Internet is a tremendous new source of information and discussion. If you structure your learning and take advantage of all that is available, you will significantly improve your chance of success.

General Poker Concepts

Afterthought

One of the factors that help keep the games good is the power of poker to generate illusions. A large portion of your opponents are quite caught up in them, looking for the hot seat, quitting to lock up a win, or maybe striving to play like some flashy fast playing opponent they perceive to be a poker phenom. These illusions should not fool *you* — not so long as you have made a reasonable study of gambling theory with an eye toward developing an appreciation for the random nature of the swings to be expected in poker. Perhaps some of the essays you have just read will have added to your clarity of thinking in these areas.

Though the topics in this section may be peripheral to the fundamentals of play in their impact on your hourly rate, with the exception of the essays on my own learning process, there is no way you can maximize your earnings without understanding them. As for how I learned poker, if anything in my experience provided ideas which some readers found useful, then those essays served their purpose.

Part Three

Strategic
Thinking in Hold 'em

Strategic
Thinking in Hold 'em

Introduction

To win at poker you must think effectively at the table. For the studious player learning to think at the table means developing the ability to put theory into practice while reading hands and opponents' thoughts. That is the focus of much of this section. I try in several essays to take you into my mind or that of a hypothetical skilled player to view some of the thought processes of poker "first hand." Of course there are many more things to think about in poker than are covered by this group of essays. They do however, provide a sampling in which both intermediate, and more advanced players, will find instructive and thought provoking.

Included are three essays on play against maniacs, not because I thought the topic was more important than others, but merely because it was on my mind at the time I wrote them. I was playing regularly then in a game notorious for the large number of tricky, experienced maniacs who frequented it. My advice on the topic thus reflects a good deal of time "in battle" with these players.

Two essays in this section were written with the express purpose, mentioned earlier, of helping players in their move up to the middle limits. The rest of the material should help with this transition as well. A caution: Make sure you have a working knowledge of bankroll requirements before settling into a higher limit on an ongoing basis. Look for extensive material on the topic by Mason Malmuth, as well as excellent essays by Sklansky.

The Strategic Moment in Hold 'em

Consider the moment when a strategic decision is made during a hand. The brief time before and during this moment finds a player assessing the relative merits of his playing options and choosing the one he deems best. Recently it occurred to me that an intermediate level player could benefit from seeing a comparison of what goes through the mind of an average player and an advanced player during these moments.[16]

Certainly each makes some sort of assessment. What separates them is the amount and nature of the information each processes in doing so. What follows is a series of comparisons in which I attempt to illustrate this difference. Each is a situation arising in the play of a hand along with examples of how an average, and an advanced player might think about it.

Note that the thought sequences attributed to the players are not intended to represent literally what goes through one's mind during a hand. Much of the thinking that I illustrate would not actually be put into words. Rather, some would take place too quickly to be verbalized to oneself, while some would exist simply as background knowledge or awareness incorporated into the decision making process, requiring little or no additional time

---

[16] I realize that there is no widely agreed upon definition in the poker world for "intermediate," "advanced," and "average." Here I use the terms as rough categories. "Intermediate" refers to a player who is somewhat better than average in skill but still has much to learn. "Advanced" refers to someone who is much better than average (but not necessarily an "expert" or a "great" player). "Average," as I see it, is a relatively unthinking, modestly losing player of only slightly developed skills.

expenditure. Nevertheless, everything that I show (and often more) would in *some* way be included in these "thoughts."

Note also, that in any of these instances, different "average" players may well have different thoughts. I merely provide what I believe would be some of the more likely possibilities. The same, of course is true of the advanced players, though not to the same degree. There are generally fewer ways to play a hand well than to play it poorly.

Finally, the "advanced" thoughts illustrated do not approach representing the highest levels of thought involved in expert poker. The hands are not unusual in nature, and the thoughts illustrated are fairly routine, unremarkable thoughts for any very good player. Moreover, the examples I provide do not necessitate much of the faster thinking that characterizes much higher level expert play. I have tried to illustrate decisions which require little more than greater knowledge of the game than that possessed by average players, and a better developed ability to think through situations at the table. By using routine examples, I hope to make the difference between how average and advanced players think during play easier to understand.

Raising Early for Value

Overview A loose, not very aggressive, full game with several players who will call two bets cold preflop, with nearly any hand they were going to play for one bet. Some of them have been doing this in an apparent effort to chase big pots. The player is under the gun holding

before the flop.

Average player's thoughts: Okay, this is a playable starting hand. Not good enough to raise with though. So I'll just call.

Advanced player's thoughts: We've had lots of multiway pots. And raises don't knock these guys out. This is a nice multiway hand. If I raise I may well get a bunch of callers and create an especially big pot. Then they'll be tied onto it if I flop a good draw. It will add a little deception to my game as well, as most of these players automatically put me on big pairs or big cards when I raise in early position. I'll raise.

Comments: Notice that the expert is aware of and thinks about more elements than the average player. In this case it enabled him to understand the situation more fully and to recognize an opportunity to which the average player was blind.

Protecting Your Hand

Overview: Again, a relatively loose game containing several "calling stations." The player holds

in the big blind. Six players limp in. The flop is:

Average player's thoughts: I have top pair. That means one thing. Gotta bet it.

Advanced player's thoughts: I have top pair but with all these players in there, and a number of possible draws my hand is extremely vulnerable. If many players stay to see the turn there's a good chance someone will draw out on me. Perhaps a check-raise would help me knock out some of these guys and protect my hand. The later positioned players here are the more aggressive. So yes, I think I should check, and hope that it's checked to one of those guys. Then when he bets I can raise and make it two bets to all the other players. That should knock out at least the long shot draws and improve my chances of winning the pot.

Comments: Once more, the advanced player covers more ground in his thinking. Here, his greater awareness of more variables and their potential impact on the hand leads him to view his options quite differently than the average player. The average player looks simplistically at little more than his general hand value. The advanced player sees the situation in more depth, considering the implications of the texture of the flop, the number and types of active players, and their positions relative to him. He then thinks about his options, settling on one which addresses the specific problem he has identified.

Inducing a Bluff

Overview: It is fifth street. The board reads:

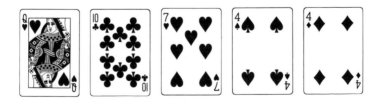

Our player holds:

He bet and was called by one player on the flop and fourth street.

Average player's thoughts: I've been betting and he's been calling all the way. No reason to think he has a four. Might as well bet again; I think I have the best hand.

Advanced player's thoughts: This guy is generally an aggressive player. I think he would surely have raised on the flop if he had a queen, or even a ten with a decent kicker. His calling all the way suggests he's probably been on a straight or flush draw. He chose to play it passively in this instance, maybe because he felt that I'd correctly put him on a draw, and would only make him pay more for it if he tried to semi-bluff or to buy a free card. I don't think there is any hand he could be holding that he would call with at this point. If I bet he'll probably just fold. But he does like to bluff if he thinks you're weak and there's some chance to pick up the pot. He might well try it here against me if I check, as he sees me as tight and knows I can lay a hand down. I think I'd do best in the long run to check and hope to induce a bluff.

Comments: We see here an average player who just throws in another bet, acting with little thought, almost on "automatic pilot." As Sklansky points out in *Poker, Gaming, & Life*, failure to think enough when heads-up on the end is common among typical players. New considerations arise on the last card, turning the decision making process there into a unique one. An advanced player knows this, and so tries to think a little more at this point in a hand. Having made the effort to acquire more knowledge, he also thinks about elements that escape the average player's purview.

The Dreaded Four Straight

Overview: The player is in a middle position in a $10-$20 game holding:

An early position player limps in, another player folds, and our player raises. Only the big blind (a generally weak player) and the limper call. The flop comes:

The player in the big blind bets out. The limper calls. Our player raises. The big blind calls, and the limper folds. The turn is the:

The big blind checks, our player bets, and the big blind calls. The river is the:

The big blind hesitates a few moments and checks.

Average player's thoughts: What a terrible card! Any ten gives him a straight. All I can do is check.

Advanced player's thoughts: Well, that queen could make a straight, but it's so obvious. He's not a sophisticated player, but he knows that I see it. If he did have the straight he'd worry that if he tried for a check-raise I'd just check behind him. He would almost definitely bet out if he did have it. I suspect he's been calling on one pair, maybe ace-little. His hesitation may have meant that he thought for a moment about trying to bet me off of my hand. But he probably decided there was too much risk of a raise, and he just wanted to show it down cheaply. My set is still good. I'm going to bet for value, and probably make more money on this hand.

Comments: Here we get a glimpse of considering what the opponent is thinking. As the example shows, average players don't do this enough. Here the average player just plays his cards. He fails to take the extra step of looking into his opponent's mind.

Note that if the advanced player were playing against another advanced player he might have had to consider checking. This is partially because he would reason, "He knows that I would expect him to bet if he did have the straight. And he knows that if he checks I may conclude he doesn't have it and may bet for value. So he may in fact have it and be going for a check-raise."

By the way, this was a hand I found in some of my old notes from past sessions. I played the hand not long after I had moved up from $6-$12 to $10-$20. Though I was certainly not a terribly advanced player, I did have an advanced *thought* in this instance.

A Multi-Purpose Semi-Bluff Raise

It's a $20-$40 game. Preflop, everyone passes to our player who is one off the button. He holds

so he raises. The button, a somewhat weak-tight player calls cold. The small blind, a normally tight, conservative, straight forward player makes it three bets. The big blind folds and both active players call. Now the flop comes:

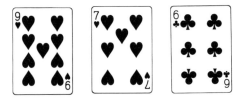

The small blind bets, our player calls, as does the button.[17] The turn brings the

The small blind again bets out.

Average player's thoughts: That ten doesn't change much. Maybe someone could have a straight, but it gives me some straight outs myself. Still, I'm mainly trying for a flush. I'll call again and hope I get there.

Advanced player's thoughts: This pot is getting sizeable. It's about to the point where I need to maximize my chance of winning it, and that ten really changes things. From their preflop play, there is little reason to think that either of these guys has an

---

[17] Astute readers will notice that the call here is debatable. A raise could be better, as it could give our player a better chance to win the pot by knocking out the player behind him, making it more likely that one pair could win for him. A raise is not, however, as clearly correct as it would be had the small blind not made it three bets preflop. This is because the great threat of a reraise from the small blind means that our player will have very little chance of picking up the pot on the flop, will have to pay an extra small bet to attempt to knock out the other player, and will probably not be given the option of taking a free card on the turn. Decisions in hold 'em are not always clear. Given the argument that *can* be made for a raise on the flop, the flop could have been the focus of this example instead of the turn. As it turns out, the decision on the turn involved very similar considerations. But certain factors were different at that point in the hand.

eight, so I'm not worried that anyone has a straight. But I can use this straight type board to apply a lot of pressure with a semi-bluff raise. The small blind might fold if he thinks I could have the straight. Also, I have three additional outs now which will probably be good if they hit. That makes the semi-bluff all the more correct. Just as important, if the guy behind me has a jack for a gut shot draw, my raise might make him fold, giving me the whole pot (instead of just half) if an eight comes on the river. Similarly, if he's calling with overcards, and has an ace with a better kicker than mine, then if I can drive him out I'll be more likely to win if I only hit an ace on the river. Yep, I'll raise.

Comments: Here is another example of thinking about elements that an average player does not consider. Pot size, the texture of the flop, reading hands (not just the board), reading the other players' potential thoughts, and other factors inform the advanced player's decision. The more thoroughly you can think through a poker problem without wasting time on irrelevant considerations, the more likely you are to come to the right answer.

This was another hand pulled from my notes. The actual result of the hand was — I am happy to report — that I caught an ace on the river to beat the small blind's

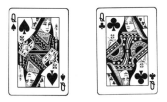

The player on the button complained that I had raised him off of

So the raise did in fact win me the pot.

Maximizing the Set

Overview: This time our player is under the gun with

in a semi-tough game. He raises and is reraised by a tight, but aggressive player immediately behind him. Everyone else folds. The flop comes:

Average player's thoughts: A set. I think I'll slowplay it till the turn. That should get me maximum profit.

Advanced player's thoughts: This guy would three-bet me before the flop with AA, KK, QQ, or AK. That makes it a little more likely that he has one of the big pairs. I want to maximize what I make on the hand on those occasions that he does have the overpair. That's where the real profit potential is here. If I can get him to misread my hand and give excessive action with an overpair, then I can make more than if I were to slowplay and give away my hand as soon as I pulled the trigger. His aggression should allow me to do that. I think the best play will be to bet out, hoping that he'll put me on a hand like

or even a draw like

Then if he raises, I'm going to reraise, and he'll either raise again, or maybe even just call, planning to raise me on the turn. If he raises again on the flop, I'll just call, then probably try to check-raise on the turn. If he just calls, (on the flop) I'll bet right into him on the turn as he expects me to, so that he can raise and I can make it three bets.

Comments: The average player uses a standard approach to the hand which, while not really bad, fails to achieve maximum profit. The advanced player adjusts to the *individual player and situation* he faces, thinking about ways to extract more money from the hand. He might have chosen a different approach, maybe even the same one used by the average player, against a less aggressive opponent, or with a different flop. Most important is that he thinks ahead in more detail than the average player. He considers his opponent's likely actions at various stages in the hand, planning ahead a sequence of actions designed to exploit them.

Final Comments

Some common elements stand out in the sample hands above. While certainly not a complete list, we can see that some of the qualities that separate the advanced player from the average player include:

1. A greater fund of knowledge. This leads to an awareness of a greater number of relevant variables and their implications in the play of a hand.
2. A more fully developed habit of thinking through situations as they arise at the table.
3. A well developed tendency to think about what opponents are thinking.
4. A better developed ability to think ahead during hands. This includes the tendency to anticipate opponents' thoughts, as well as their actions.
5. A greater sensitivity to the need for situational, player specific adjustments.

These are but some of the abilities that you can develop or strengthen through serious study of the game. I hope you see that the payoff makes it worth the effort. And if you are already beyond the "advanced" level illustrated, you know that even the effort to learn just a little more can pay off better than most players imagine.

One Way Not to Fold

Warning: *This article could be dangerous for the average player.* Typically, such a player not only plays too many hands, but goes too far with them. Where he probably needs the most help is in learning when to fold. Yet this essay is more about how *not* to fold. I am going to discuss one way to take a hand of little obvious worth and win a pot *on the worth* of that hand. It's a kind of play, well known to advanced players, which I hope will stimulate thought and further learning for ambitious intermediate players; for it illustrates some important considerations which come up all the time in poker:

1. A fundamental principle of poker is that hand values are always relative. You need only enough to win. A pair with a king kicker beats the same pair with a queen kicker as surely as a straight flush beats a ten-high no pair.

2. All players can benefit from honing the kind of flexibly quick thinking which, if you have developed it through practice and thinking about poker away from the game, can help you seize profitable opportunities that other players might miss.

3. Positional betting tactics are often a key to maximizing your expectation in a hand.

Studious readers will recognize that the play I will discuss is similar to one involving the play of top pair with a small kicker which is described in the chapter on the free card in Sklansky and Malmuth's *Hold 'em Poker for Advanced Players: 21st Century Edition*. It may, in fact, be that the first edition of that book provided my first exposure to the logical basis for the play. This illustrates how most plays and concepts in poker can be extended to new situations, and can be adjusted to create new plays. If you do enough thinking about poker, you can even use ideas you learn as springboards to uncover new concepts of which you were previously unaware. As a thinking player, you should strive in this way to use newly acquired ideas and concepts as stimuli for further learning.

The Situation

Consider this scenario: You are in the big blind in a $20-$40 hold 'em game with a weak hand:

A loose player of average ability limps in under the gun. A weak-tight player, and a loose, passive type call in middle positions. Finally, the button, a loose, aggressive player calls, followed by an average player in the small blind. (As an aside, this is a good time to feel fortunate. In my games, a free play in the big blind is as rare as good television.)

There is $120 in the pot as you take the flop six-handed. Now the flop comes:

Despite your pair, given the looseness of your opponents, you can't like this flop very much. If you bet and are not raised you will almost surely be called, probably in two or three places. It will be difficult to narrow down the callers' hands, and the fourth street card may well negate your already modest winning possibilities. Against fewer opponents or a different lineup of players a bet could make more sense. Here, though perhaps close, it is likely to be unprofitable. Checking and folding most of the time in this spot is hard to criticize.

So let's say that when the small blind checks, you check along. Now the next three limpers also check. You begin to wonder if you may, in fact, have the best hand. You start to hope for some innocuous card on fourth street, but now the guy on the button, true to his aggressive nature, bets. The small blind folds and it's up to you again. Do you see what has happened? If you have worked on your ability to make quick revisions in your assessments of hands and situations as they play out, then you will recognize that things have changed. (In this situation, more experienced, advanced players are aware of the possibility well before it happens.) A few seconds ago you had little in the way of a hand. Suddenly you have a very real shot at this pot. Here's what you must consider. If any of the first three players behind you had a jack, there's a good chance they'd have bet. (There's some chance they'd have bet an eight as well.) As for the button, because of the way he plays he'll probably bet all sorts of hands including middle pair, bottom pair, a gut shot draw, or even a pure bluff. Given the large number of hands he will bet, your hand figures to be better than his at this point. Just as importantly, indications are that none of the other players has a strong enough hand to call a raise cold.

The Play

Your decision is clear. Instead of folding as you had more or less expected to do at the outset of the hand, you now *raise*. By raising the late position bettor you are able to confront the players between him and you with having to call two bets cold to stay in the hand. From there on the hand may develop in a variety of ways, but frequently from that point through fourth street your hand plays itself. Ideally, and commonly, your raise will knock the other players out. Your standard play, if you are called on the flop (preferably only by the button), is to bet again on fourth street. If instead you are reraised on the flop the pot will be big enough that you should generally call that bet, but frequently be prepared to fold on the turn unless you improve. Once someone makes it three bets, going beyond the turn without improvement would be reckless unless you have an excellent read to the contrary, or the raiser is quite a maniac. This is especially true if the reraiser is one of the players between you and the original bettor.

The river can be a bit more tricky. Let's assume it's now heads-up between you and the button, and the last card appears unlikely to have helped his hand. You must now decide whether to bet or to check and call. (Given the opponent I described, it is clear enough that your hand is worth a call if you check and he bets. Of course in the real world you have to assess each situation individually.) At a minimum you must ask yourself what range of hands your opponent will call (or raise) with if you bet, and what hands he will bet if you check. You then bet or check and call on the basis of which play would give you the highest proportion of wins in the long run. This is actually a complex topic which I will leave to the ambitious reader to study in some depth in David Sklansky's *The Theory of Poker*. As a quick rule of thumb, however, lean toward betting if — as with many weak and mediocre players — he will call with more hands than he would bet if you were to check. Be more inclined to check and call if — as with some more aggressive or bluff-prone players — he will bet with more hands than he would call with. (Also, check if you are concerned that he may bluff-raise.)

Note that had the flop come

your considerations would be slightly different. You might now give more thought to betting out on the flop, as you cannot easily be called by overcards. In many games it is also now less likely that anyone holds top pair.

The Concepts

Central to this play is having a late position bettor who will bet all sorts of hands less than top pair.[18] Note that even if he has the same pair you do, but with a better kicker, he may fold (probably on fourth street) in response to the strength you've shown with your check-raise. It is your check-raise which gives you the leverage to drive out the other players. Most rational players will fold for two bets with anything less than top pair with a good kicker or a solid draw. Better players will often fold top pair. Of course, you sometimes run into a good hand and have to fold. But if you never make this play you are giving up a bit of profit.

It is crucial to realize that while the leverage of the check-raise in powering out potentially better hands may be dramatic, this play's essence is really the recognition that your hand has greater value, relative to the other hands in play, than you could

---

[18] It is important that the other players not be fully aware of this propensity of his, or your play could backfire. This is because they may be checking better hands than yours behind you.

have assumed just moments before. For the less than expert player, if this recognition comes at all, it will often be in the form of a sudden realization during the hand. You are more likely to have such realizations if you nurture the flexibly quick thinking mentioned at the beginning of this article. Doing this begins with your study of poker theory and thinking about hands away from the table. Add to that the practice of focusing intensely on the dynamics of hands as they play out, striving to identify the most important variables of play, and to apply theory to the real life play situations you observe. Then, with experience and study, this and other situations will become familiar to you. You will actually anticipate them before they arise. Still, no matter how much you commit to memory, the ability to make rapid shifts in your thinking, remaining open to the possibility of changes in relative hand strength, is a valuable skill to hone as you advance in poker. It will enable you to spot additional, less frequently occurring, hidden opportunities for profit as you play. It is thus one of the marks of the expert.

Conclusion and *Caution*

Think about the example I have provided, not just as a trick to add to your arsenal, but as it illustrates the importance of being aware of the relative nature of hand values. Consider also the value of being ready to adjust your thinking about a hand as the unfolding action provides you with new information. Use this play, as well, to stimulate further thinking about positional tactics. Then you will move beyond playing by rote, into applying a deeper understanding of poker to your day to day play.

Bear in mind that this sort of play requires good judgement. As I mentioned, an awareness of the utility of this tactic could prove dangerous for the player lacking such judgement, or sufficient discipline. There are lots of semi-skilled, losing players who know this and all sorts of other similar plays. One reason they lose is because they apply them constantly and indiscriminately. They generally play too fast. Don't get carried away making a move like this every time you have a pair in an early position and the last person bets. Even the best players misread this situation sometimes. When they do they run into big hands, or get trapped for a couple of bets more than they should. However, their judgment generally allows them to stay out of trouble and lose less than others would when they guess wrong. So make this play only when it is *clear* that the circumstances are right. Indiscriminate application of ideas like this one will prove costly. Prudent, selective application, on the other hand, can be one profitable way *not* to fold.

Beating the Berserko:
Preflop Against a Maniac

The mind of the maniac is a curious thing. As a one time psychotherapist, I am intrigued by and a little sympathetic toward the emotional disturbance reflected in the markedly aberrant behavior of the maniac at the poker table. But being now primarily a poker player, I will undertake no analysis of the psyche of this kind of player. I will present only some ideas, intended to elaborate on what has been covered elsewhere in the poker literature concerning how to play against this troubled, but troublesome opponent. So let's dig beneath the surface a little to explore some of the conceptual underpinnings of a correct preflop anti-maniac strategy.

The Debate Over Where to Sit

Whether you want a maniac on your right or left has been the subject of some debate. On the Internet, for example, players often argue the merits of each option. The reason each has merits is because either can be the best choice depending on the conditions of the game in which you find yourself. As Sklansky and Malmuth explain in *Hold 'em Poker for Advanced Players: 21st Century Edition*, the time when other players in the game are going to interfere with the normal strategy you employ is when he is on your right. That is, if you are close to the maniac's immediate left, and reraise him preflop, you want to be able to drive out the players behind you in order to isolate him. But when players in your game will come in behind you with less than great hands despite your making it three bets, this strategy is ruined. In that case you can opt to put the maniac on your immediate left so that you can check to him, let him bet, then see how the rest of the players react before deciding how to play your hand. This is advantageous since it is somewhat akin to giving yourself last position.

Though the tactic of placing the maniac on your left does have its place, I lean toward placing him on my right far more often. One reason for this is that as long as I do not carry it to an extreme, in the games I play in, three-betting a maniac usually does effectively knock out the players behind me. Not carrying it to an extreme means, for instance, not three-betting too liberally in earlier positions, and not often playing against him with the weaker end of the spectrum of hands which should theoretically show a profit against a typical maniac. Trying to play every possible hand against him runs the risk of increasing the frequency with which you are seen trying to isolate him, causing opponents to start jumping in and spoiling your plans.

There is another reason I usually favor keeping a maniac on my right. The strategy of putting the maniac on your left should work best against an extremely consistent, predictable maniac. If he raises preflop, and bets after the flop nearly every chance he gets, then by putting him on your left you do get the advantages of putting everyone else between you and the maniac before deciding what to do, but I seem rarely to encounter such a predictable maniac. More often I have run into players who might be termed "semi-maniacs." They essentially qualify as maniacs, but do have some mix to their play, do not play every hand, and sometimes just limp in. In addition, though they are aggressive after the flop, they are also capable of laying a hand down, and cannot simply be counted on to bet into the field for you. Because much of the advantage of sitting to his right is therefore lost, I prefer to sit to the left of this sort of maniac.[19] Of course this may have to do with the particular games I have played in. You need to determine what kind of maniac you are dealing with, and how the other players are going to respond to you before deciding

---

[19] Notice that in no-limit or pot-limit games the edge afforded by having someone who will bet often on your left is much greater.

where to sit. Nevertheless, for the rest of this essay and the two related essays to follow, I will address playing only with the maniac on your right.

Hand Selection and Preflop Play

The remaining questions against a maniac before the flop are what kinds of hands to play and how to play them. Most players do a poor job of hand selection in this spot. For instance, when sitting to the maniac's left, many worry that his raising with so many hands will force them out of too many pots. So they opt to loosen up on their cold calls and simply play for two bets against his raise with any hand they would normally limp in with, while perhaps reraising with their best hands. While this may approach being correct with some hands in *some* games, against some extreme preflop maniacs who become more passive and play weakly after the flop, more precise hand selection is normally required, especially in earlier positions. The simplistic "ignore his raises" approach probably stems from their failure to consider the maniac's effects on the other players in the game, and to extend their thinking to play after the flop.[20]

In a ring game you must think about the maniac's play *in the context* of the ring game. If you play too many hands against a maniac in earlier positions, in a game containing skilled aggressive players, you may find that it won't matter that your starting hands are better on average than the maniac's. When tough players reraise behind you it will cost you three bets to play mediocre hands, wedged between a maniac and a tough player. Without the maniac in the game, you might limp in with those

---

[20] This is an example of what I believe is a common flaw in how many players think about poker and make their playing decisions. They take note of one element in isolation — a maniac is raising before the flop — and fail to look for its impact on or relation to other aspects of the game.

hands, but then would have to pay only two bets to see the flop when someone raises, and would not have to contend with both a maniac and a tough player.

More generally, the number of hands you play against a maniac should be influenced by your assessment of the other players in the game. How aggressive are they? How deceptive? How much respect do they accord your raises? How are they responding to the maniac? How do they think you are responding to him? Are other players getting caught up in the maniac's action and calling loosely behind you, even for two or three bets? Such questions will play a big part in hand selection decisions.

It is also crucial to consider the implications of the maniac's play after the flop. Many hands do not play well heads-up after the flop against a classic maniac's relentless, aggressive style of play. This is another reason to often avoid playing hands like

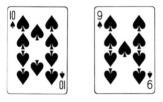

or

in early position behind a maniac's raise. (An exception might be in an otherwise loose, passive game in which you can confidently expect several callers, but not reraisers behind you if you call.) Rather, you need to shift hand selection toward hands that can go to the river with a realistic chance of winning unimproved. In early positions these include hands like

and

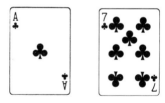

As your position improves you can add additional hands containing aces or kings, and slightly smaller pocket pairs. Play these hands usually by reraising to isolate the maniac, playing him heads-up after the flop. Note that this means you will be playing more hands against the maniac's raises than you would against the raises of a "normal" player. But be careful not to make the common mistake of going too far with this. You will not be giving up much, and may save a good deal, if you always fold a hand like

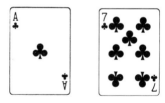

behind a maniac's raise, regardless of your position, just as you would against any other player.

What you are doing here is very profitable since you are consistently creating a large hand strength differential by pitting your good hands only against the maniac's (on average) weak hands. Moreover, you do this by knocking other players out, which you accomplish through the very act of investing more money (reraising) in that hand strength differential.

Against maniacs who play and raise with nearly every hand, but then become more passive after the flop, you can begin to add more hands like the T♠9♠ and Q♦T♦ mentioned above. But for the most part, unless you are an expert and are playing against a maniac who plays weakly after the flop, and are against an otherwise soft lineup, I suggest you add these hands only in later positions. Even then, you may want to restrict your play of such hands to those times when other players have limped in ahead of the maniac (and you do not expect them to reraise him) so that a multiway pot is guaranteed. Also, in my experience only a minority of maniacs fit this description (loose and aggressive before the flop, more passive afterward). When you do play such hands, however, you should not necessarily reraise, particularly if anyone has come in ahead of the maniac. Such hands play well multiway, and by sometimes just calling the maniac you avoid punishing him so severely for his raising that he begins to play better. His excessive raising does, after all, present you with a profitable opportunity.

Another reason to get the pot heads-up, overlooked by most players, is that the more skilled maniac can be quite adept at leveraging his hand on a later street by raising the third player's bets. The effect can be to force you out when you hold the best hand. By playing him heads-up, you deprive him at least of this method of taking the pot away from you.

As mentioned above there are times when conditions will be different from those I have assumed here. Little in poker is carved in stone. There are other occasions, for instance, when it makes sense not to reraise the maniac. Obviously, if you are several seats to his left and players come in between the two of you, you cannot make the same use of the reraise that I have described here. Even on his immediate left, just calling is sometimes best, even with hands that play very well heads-up. You might be holding big suited cards, for example, in a game in which most of the players have been calling two bets with anything they would normally limp in with. Here just calling will allow you to pick up lots of players to pay you off if you hit a big draw. It also further mitigates the problem of punishing the maniac so often that he adjusts.

Though there is much more to consider, I have tried to provide a good sample of things you must think about in order to understand in any depth how to play before the flop against a maniac. A major reason for paying so much attention to proper hand selection against a maniac is that it goes a long way towards keeping you out of tough spots after the flop. In the next essay I will address playing against a maniac after the flop.

On Into
the Storm: Playing
the Maniac After the Flop

In this essay my focus will be on play after the flop — on into the storm, if you will, of a hand played against a maniac. Once again, my aim is to go a little beyond what the poker literature has said about this topic to date.

There are Maniacs,
and Then There are Maniacs

It has been my experience that maniacs vary more in their play after the flop than they do preflop. Two reasons for this stand out: First, hold 'em itself becomes more varied, more complex after the flop. From that point on, the maniac is responding to more complexities in the cards, is faced with more intricate decisions (even if he does tend to approach them one dimensionally), and has more playing options available to him. Second, fourth street separates those maniacs who are truly willing to blow off a lot of money from the sizable percentage who suddenly acquire some prudence when the bet doubles.

After the flop you may be faced with a maniac who remains hyperaggressive throughout the hand, or one who calms down on the turn. He may play in a straight forward fashion or may be deceptive. He may play much better than he did preflop. Some maniacs exhibit surprising flashes of sophistication in their play on the later streets. Others are unthinking all the way through. Therefore, as is so often the case in poker problems, you must know your player in order to make the best decisions against him.

144

Anti-Maniac Strategy

That said, we can nevertheless identify some strategic maneuvers that are useful against the "typical" maniac. Let's assume that he plays very agressively on the flop, that he will continue betting through the river, but that he often slows down when raised on the turn. For the sake of this discussion let's also assume that you are heads-up against the maniac. This will often be the case if you are seated to his left and have reraised him before the flop.

A key concept in dealing with a maniac is that of using his aggression to your own advantage. If you keep this in mind as you read the rest of this essay, every tactic I suggest should be easy to understand.

Big Hands, Little Hands, and In-Between Hands

Now assume you are heads-up and have flopped a big hand such as a set without many drawing possibilities present for your opponent. This is a nice situation. Your main concern is simply getting as much money as possible into the pot. If your maniac is one of those who is willing to invest a ridiculous number of bets on the flop with a mediocre hand, then you should probably keep raising right there until he finally stops, or you become concerned that he may have you beat (if your hand is not the nuts). Some maniacs will keep raising enough on the flop that the money to be made there outweighs whatever you could expect to make by stopping sooner on the flop, in order to get a raise in on the turn. (However, you might want to think about how playing in this manner, intended to extract as much money as possible on *this* hand, will affect the maniac's play against you on future hands. Sometimes this may point to a different approach.)

If you are against someone who thinks a little more about the meaning of your continued raising, you have to be looking for the point at which he will back off on his aggression and simply call you down, or even fold. There you will need to gauge whether or not you could collect more by slowplaying a little on the flop, and waiting for the turn (or the river) to raise. Note that a key to this is the likelihood that he will call your fourth street raise. Even with this approach, against many maniacs you will have little trouble working in three bets on the flop, without jeopardizing your chance to raise on the turn.

You need to make a similar decision when dealing with the kind of maniac who remains very aggressive on the turn. Against him you will often make more by getting the bets in on the turn. However, you will be unable to do this if you have shown too much aggression on the flop, thereby tipping him off to the strength of your hand.

What about a hand at the other end of the playable spectrum? It is not unusual against a maniac to find yourself holding what may well be the best hand with something like bottom pair or ace-high. Here you must know your player. If you know he will automatically bluff or bet something worse than your hand, then you can take the approach of letting him bet for you. By checking and calling (or merely calling when you are behind him) you give him the opportunity to bluff off his money all the way through the hand. Moreover, you avoid being raised while playing a vulnerable holding.

You must read him as best you can though, considering anything you know about what kind of hand he may have played given his position and actions before the flop, and relating this to his subsequent actions and the board as it develops. Bottom pair on a flop of

does not play the same as bottom pair on a flop of

You might sometimes play to the river with the latter, but must much more often fold the former.

In between the strong and marginal hands I have discussed there are many hands such as top pair with a reasonable kicker, and two pair. With these decent but not tremendous hands you must adapt your play to the player and the situation. For example, there are times when acting on what you know about your opponent's tendencies, you might play top pair very aggressively, while waiting until the turn or even the river to raise. Then there are times when you might revert to checking and calling even with two pair after being raised just once on the flop. It all depends on your opponent and what you read him for.

On the River, and Reading the Maniac

If you do play a hand with a check and call approach you should nevertheless consider the pros and cons of betting out on fifth street. The decision on the last card is unique, and betting rather than checking will sometimes be correct. Also, when you bet for value on the river in this situation and are not called, you have not always lost as much as it appears when you consider only that your opponent may have been induced to bluff had you checked. This is because when he does fold, you have at least kept your strategy concealed. He does not see your cards, so you have not revealed your check and call approach to your opponent. He will thus be less likely to adapt to it by reducing his bluffing frequency in the future.

Remember that just because you are up against a player who bluffs way too often and can usually be counted on to play aggressively, does not mean that you can abandon the thinking and analysis that you normally put into playing a hand. Don't do what many mediocre players do. They peg someone as a habitual bluffer, and call him down unthinkingly any time they have anything in the neighborhood of ace high or better, no matter how the board develops, and no matter how the opponent may have recently adjusted his play. Frequently, it is obvious that they are throwing their money away, for some maniacs do think and do not always bet without anything. Furthermore, it is not at all uncommon for a maniac to vary his play during a session. Sometimes he does so as a strategic maneuver, while other times it may be a response to how much he is winning or losing.

I can think of one maniac with whom I've played many times. I made a lot of money against this player, but I was always amazed to see how well he survived at poker despite his extreme play. His secret (of which I'm not sure he was actually aware himself) was that players so often gave him grossly excessive action, always assuming that he had nothing. Yes, they frequently picked off his bluffs, but they also paid him off all the way far more frequently than they should have. Even worse, they too often took something like top pair with a mediocre kicker and engaged in raising wars with him. They were not sufficiently attuned to his play to detect when he was more likely to have a real hand or when his raises had surpassed what he would be willing to do with his bluffs or semi-bluffs. He thus pulled in a lot of pots that were pumped up by multiple wasted bets from his opponents.

You must keep reading the maniac's hand despite his irrational starting standards. Those players who figure that hand reading is fruitless against a maniac because "he could have anything" are giving up an important part of their edge on such a player. Though he may be difficult to read, if you take what you do know about his starting standards, betting patterns and tendencies, watch the board as it develops, and observe for tells, you *will* gain useful information to use in play against such an "unpredictable" opponent. If you combine this with using his aggression against him, keeping in mind the ideas laid out above, you should have a solid foundation for your journey "into the storm."

One Reason to Reraise a Maniac

Suppose you are playing in a game containing a maniac who is seated close to your right. We'll call him Fred. I'll specify that he is a maniac who usually remains overly aggressive throughout a hand. Now suppose someone limps in from an early position before the flop. Fred raises from an early-middle position, and you just call in a middle position with:

A third guy, a weak but somewhat erratic player whom we'll call Jake calls the two bets cold behind you. The big blind folds. The limper and Fred call making this a four way pot. The flop comes

giving you the top two pair. The first guy checks. Fred bets out. You figure he could have a flush draw, an ace with any sort of kicker, a gut shot draw with or without a pair, two pair, a pair of queens or jacks with which he's hoping somehow to win, a straight, or a set. Knowing Fred, the weaker possibilities are not at all unlikely. You probably have the best hand, so you raise. Jake calls cold behind you. You believe he would make such a

150

call with any ace, a flush draw, two pair, or a gutshot draw. You doubt he would slowplay the straight or a set, so you see those hands as unlikely for him. The first player folds and Fred calls. It is now a three way pot. At this point you like your hand.

On the turn comes the

a bad card for you as any king now beats you. Fred checks. Does that mean he doesn't have a king, or does he have one and is trying to check-raise? Though exactly what you should do now is debatable, let's say you reasonably decide to check along. Now Jake bets. Not good, but if Fred folds or just calls, thereby ruling out the straight for him, you plan to call. You fear that Jake has a king, but you know he is an unthinking player. You have several times seen him bet a flush draw when it's checked to him on fourth street, no matter what the previous action, oblivious to how threatening the board is. He could be betting two pair as well, perhaps thinking, "Well, they checked so I must have them beat." These possibilities plus your chance of filling up on the river would dictate a call, given the 8.5-to-1 or 9.5-to-1 pot odds you'll be getting. But now the action is on Fred. He raises. "Wonderful," you think sarcastically. He appears to have the straight. Alternatively, he could have spiked a set of tens. He might well raise with them here.

But this is Fred; he is a maniac and is quite capable of overplaying something like two pair in this spot. He is an excessive bluffer who could even have nothing but a pair, thinking that he can steal the pot if no one has a straight, using the scary board as leverage. You could realistically have him beat. If you were head up against just Fred you would go to the river. But against two players showing strength it looks bad for you.

Moreover, instead of calling one big bet with pot odds of about 9.5-to-1, you are now faced with the prospect of calling two bets (with the added possibility of another raise coming from Jake) getting little more than 5-to-1. You quite reasonably decide to fold, but you do so with the nagging recognition that Fred's raise in this spot may not have meant the same thing as a raise from a "normal" player. Now Jake calls Fred's raise. The river is a blank. Both players check. That gives you a sinking feeling. Jake turns over a

Fred shows

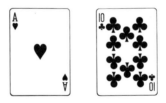

and takes the pot. So his aggressive play forced you out with the best hand, leaving him to beat the worst hand.

   Frustrating outcomes like this are not unusual when playing against maniacs in multiway pots. But in this hypothetical example, playing slightly differently might save you the pot. First consider the kind of hand you have. More often than not, A♦Q♥ is not even worth playing against a raise, but against a typical maniac it is so likely to be superior to his hand that you should certainly play. However, note that A♦Q♥ is a one pair type of hand. You are generally hoping to flop top pair and have it hold up to win the pot. This is contrasted with a hand like

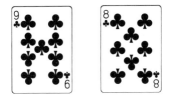

which is far less likely to win with one pair, but more likely to make a straight or a flush. One pair has a much smaller chance of holding up when pitted against multiple opponents. When they are all drawing to different hands, there is a good chance one of them is going to get there. So with a hand like A♦Q♥ it is generally advisable to eliminate other players so that you can play your hand against a small number of opponents.[21]

Beyond the advantages of thinning the field with a one pair type of hand, getting it heads-up against a maniac can eliminate the kinds of trouble in which you found yourself against Fred and Jake. To illustrate, let's say that instead of just calling Fred's preflop raise, you reraise him. Now Jake is almost sure not to call with his J♣T♥. (If he *is* going to call three bets cold with J♣T♥, then he is such a bad player that if you have to have someone else in on this hand he's the kind of player you want.) To be realistic, we'll assume the limper goes ahead and calls the two additional bets to him. Though he might not, such calls seem to be the norm in many games (especially given that he has to expect at least one raise behind him). Fred, of course will at least call. So now it's a three way pot *without* anyone behind you. On the flop Fred bets, you raise, the limper folds as before, and Fred calls. It's now a two way pot, making the turn much easier to play. Though the absence of the third player could cause Fred to play differently, let's say his actions are the same now as in the multiway scenario: He checks, hoping to raise. Though you too might consider a different play (betting) in this as contrasted with the multiway situation,

---

[21] What I have described is not the only important reason to try to get it head up with a hand like A♦Q♥. See the essay, "Beating the Berzerko: Preflop Against a Maniac" for more.

we'll assume you check along so as to avoid a check-raise and take a free card with this threatening board. On the river it is quite possible that Fred will bet, seeing your check on the turn as a sign that he probably has the best hand. You, of course, have an easy call.

Notice that the lack of the third player completely prevented you from being faced with difficult decisions. It is obviously on difficult decisions that you are most likely to make costly errors. In this case you win a decent size pot which Fred would have taken away from you in the multiway scenario. That's a costly error avoided.

I have illustrated here a major benefit that can accrue from reraising a maniac. There are others as well, some of which I touched on in the essay, "Beating the Berzerko: Preflop Against a Maniac." Note, however, that while a reraise is often the preflop play of choice against a player like Fred, it does have its limits. I have seen many good players who virtually *always* reraise a maniac. This is wrong. It is a response which stems from a failure to think enough about individual hands as well as their larger strategy in the game as a whole. There are situations which dictate a call rather than a reraise. To mention just one, suppose you are in a middle position holding a hand like

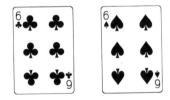

and the maniac on your immediate right raises three limpers of varying ability. Your small pair is generally playable here, but a reraise would probably be a bad idea. If you don't think you can knock out everyone behind you as well as all the limpers, then a call makes much more sense.

There are other situations in which you may have a borderline decision between reraising and just calling. On these occasions you might want to consider that if you *too* often punish a maniac with reraises before the flop, he may actually adjust his play and stop making as many incorrect raises. Do you want him to start playing better? What's more, you don't want the other players in the game to become inured to, and start disregarding your reraises. So with good hands that do better multiway for instance, consider just calling some portion of the time.

A Simple Read

Reading hands is one of the key skills that must be well developed for a player to succeed above the smaller limit games. Two key facets of hand reading in hold 'em are:

1. Interpreting your opponent's actions on each betting round, and narrowing down the hand he might have, in light of the cards that have been dealt up to that point.
2. Looking backward from the current point in the hand to interpret the meaning of your opponent's action in light of the previous cards, and his previous actions.

As you can probably see, these two elements are closely intertwined. In practice they will often be indistinguishable as parts of the hand reading process as a whole, but for purposes of study it is useful to separate them.

For more discussion of these and other aspects of reading hands I refer you to Sklansky and Malmuth's *Hold 'em Poker for Advanced Players: 21st Century Edition* as well as *The Theory of Poker* and *Hold 'em Poker* both by David Sklansky.

A Bet From Out of Nowhere

To demonstrate these points I will describe a read from a hand I played. It clearly illustrates the process of eliminating hands your opponent might have by interpreting his actions as the hand progresses and successive cards are dealt. It is also an example of looking back to see what his action on the end might indicate in light of his previous actions in the hand. This hand took place in a $40-$80 hold 'em game which was about average for a game at this limit in Southern California with regard to its overall level of tightness and aggression. I will not explain the thinking behind my actions throughout the hand. That is beyond the scope of this essay. Here I will focus only on my read of my opponent's hand.

I was in the small blind holding:

Everyone folded and I completed the small blind for $20. (Note that this game is played with a time charge rather than a rake or drop. Therefore many of the players, including myself, opt not to "chop" in the blinds.) The big blind, who is normally very aggressive in such heads-up situations did not raise. The flop came:

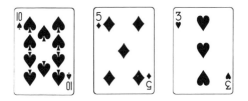

I checked, and he checked along. Because he was not only an aggressive player, but a tricky one, this told me that he either had very little, perhaps just two low cards without much relation to the flop, or he was slowplaying something fairly strong. The turn brought the

Again we both checked. Now I knew he almost certainly had nothing. In fact, I knew I very likely had the best hand. Do you see why? If not, you might want to pause here for a moment to think about how I could have concluded that my hand was likely best.

The river was the

This time I checked and he bet. It was like a bet from out of nowhere. Why? Well, I knew this player well enough to know that he almost surely would have bet earlier in the hand with any pair. He also would have bet with ace-high most of the time. He was savvy enough to know that such a bet could have merit either as a bet for value or as a semi-bluff. Therefore, it was very unlikely that he had an ace *or* any other pair. Nor did I fear a better king-high. All but one of them would give him two overcards with which he would have raised preflop and bet after the flop, or a gutshot draw on the turn which he also would likely have bet. This made my king-high a strong favorite to be the best hand.

So what did my opponent's bet mean? Well, just as I had noticed his checking on every previous round, and had concluded that he held a very weak hand, he had noticed mine. He knew that my checks suggested a weak hand for me as well. He figured I probably couldn't call a bet (and assumed I was unlikely to check-raise as a bluff), and thus reasoned he had a good chance to pick up the pot with a bet. I therefore put him fairly confidently on a bluff. So I called with my relatively "good" no pair hand, despite getting only 2-to-1 from the pot. He showed

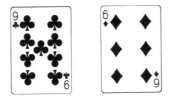

and I took the pot.

Notice that this read was made simpler by the hand being played heads-up. With additional players involved, not only might I have had to read other hands, but I would have been less sure of my read of this opponent's hand. For instance, he probably would have been a little less likely to bet before the river with something like a small pair or ace-high.

The two skills I have highlighted here are important to develop in order to be a good reader. Work on eliminating hands as you relate your opponent's actions on each round to the cards that have come. Look back from the current round through all previous rounds to see how his current action makes sense when related to the previous cards and actions. Hint: As was the case with this hand, you will sometimes spot a bluff because his current action does *not* make much sense in that light.

Countering a Good Reader

In poker, once you move beyond the fundamentals, reading hands becomes a hugely important area of play. Top players and authors generally agree that reading hands may be the single most important advanced skill. It is coupled closely with reading opponents' thoughts — what Sklansky refers to in *The Theory of Poker* when he explains the process of thinking about what your opponent is thinking. Accordingly, there is a clear positive correlation between players' skill levels and their reading abilities. In other words, better players tend to be better readers, and their reads make them money. They use them to save money on losing hands, and make more money on winning hands.

Thus, when you play against such players you must counter their reading abilities. You do this, in large part, with your own reading skills. You read their hand, assess what they read you for (reading their read, if you will) and apply deception. The purpose of the deception is to make them put you on the wrong hand. You thus *manipulate* their read, leading them to play their hand differently from how they would if they read you correctly. This of course, makes you money. Often, against tougher players, the kinds of deception I am talking about go beyond routine and well known plays like raising for a free card or semi-bluffing with a draw.

Inducing the Wrong Read to Trigger Excessive Action

Here's a hand I played which provides an unusually clear example of these ideas. It was a full, nine-handed $40-$80 hold 'em game which had been largely unremarkable. A short while earlier Bill had taken a seat in the game. He's a player who is more skilled than most, but he does have one key weakness:

Though advanced in his hand reading ability, he often fixes rigidly on a specific read, having trouble revising it in the face of contradictory evidence. This is especially costly for him because it often leads him to go too far with aggressive bluffing and semi-bluffing when he thinks he has a good read on an opponent's hand. On this day he had another problem as well. He appeared to have come into the game slightly on tilt. I wasn't sure why, but he had played even more aggressively than usual, to the point of recklessness, from the moment he joined the game.

I was in the big blind. Sitting two seats to my left, Bill called before the flop. Ted, on Bill's immediate left, also called. He is a loose, aggressive, generally mediocre player. An unfamiliar player on the button raised. This player had been raising before the flop with a remarkably wide range of hands and betting until he met resistance after the flop. I looked down and saw:

Believing I had little chance of knocking out Bill or Ted by reraising, I called and we took the flop four-handed.

The flop was excellent for me:

Although I liked this flop, it was not immediately obvious how best to play my hand against these players. With that flop, I could only expect play from someone who had one or two sixes, a king, AA, a flush draw, an in-between pair like 88, or someone who might make it beyond the flop to pick up a pair or a draw on the turn. If anyone did have 66, a king, a flush draw, or AA I would not lose him on the flop.

I could try to slowplay until the turn, but in addition to the two-suited flop, there was the near certainty that the player on the button was going to bet anyway. When he did there would be few hands with which Bill or Ted would call (or raise) one, but not two bets. Thus, I didn't have to worry about knocking out anyone who was going to call one bet anyway. I could bet out and hope not to lose everyone. Maybe I would even be raised. Since I usually play against people who are familiar with me, I like to mix it up a bit in spots like this. I want my opponents to be uncertain or to misread my hand on a paired flop. That's what led me to my third option. Given Bill's propensity for very aggressive action based on sophisticated, logical, but rigid reads, I suspected I might have an opportunity to induce excessive action from him. It required that I convince him that I did *not* have the trips.

Of course it might turn out that any action would come from one of the other two players but, aiming to carry out my plan to draw unwarranted aggression from Bill, I checked. As I expected, it was checked to the preflop raiser who bet. Then came the centerpiece of my plan. I raised. Now, check-raising a player on your right from an early position will frequently have the effect of knocking out players in between the two of you. Often you do it to protect a vulnerable hand like top pair in a multiway pot. *I knew Bill knew that.* I also knew that he knew I was a player who could lay down a hand less than trips if I thought *he* had them. So my hope was that he would read me for having a hand like

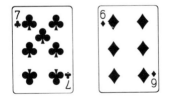

or

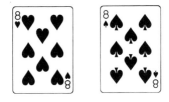

which I wanted to protect, and that he would try to bluff or semi-bluff me off of it.

I was helped by the presence of the player on the button. I knew Bill had seen that this was not only a poor player, but one who would always bet if everyone checked to him on the flop. I knew this would encourage Bill to assume I would be especially likely to try to isolate this player without much of a hand. I felt also that his apparent tilt would add to his willingness to gamble on a bold steal attempt.

Well, gamble he did. When I check-raised, Bill three-bet it. Ted called all three bets cold, and the button folded. Now, here I could have just called, perhaps with a plan to check-raise on the turn. Under typical circumstances that would have been worth considering. But, while I couldn't be certain of it, my guess was that by maintaining my aggressive stance on the flop, as if I were "representing" rather than actually holding the trips, I could get even more action out of Bill. It would work as long as he held firmly to his read. Since I thought he would, I capped it at four bets. He and Ted called. The turn was the 9s. I bet right out, and Bill raised again. Ted called the two bets cold. I knew Ted would be very unlikely to slowplay a full house at this point in the hand. Furthermore, I knew him well, and saw in his demeanor indicators to suggest that he was simply calling all bets, trying to make his hand. I put him on a flush draw.

With his turn raise, Bill had pushed his hand hard. Ironically, though it was exactly what I had wanted him to do, he had now shown so much aggression that I had to consider whether he might in fact have a hand which beat me, such as

or

From what I knew of his play, I believed he would have slowplayed a pair of sixes on the flop. The K♦9♦ was possible, but I believed that his misreading my hand combined with his emotional state could as easily account for his action. I felt his actions would have been the same with either the case king alone or a flush draw. That made one of the those hands far more likely than the K♦9♦. In short, I was fairly sure I had been able to prompt him to semi-bluff twice in a hopeless attempt to make me lay down my apparent "weak" hand. I therefore made it three bets. Both players called, partially confirming my read on Bill. Had he had me beaten, he probably would have raised again right there. The river was the 4♦. I bet and both players folded, confirming busted flush draws for both of them.

So, I'd induced Bill to spend about six small bets (an additional $240) more than he had to in playing his hand. I was just lucky that Ted had the hand he did, and came along for the ride as well. Of course, I cannot be sure how Bill would have responded had I played my hand differently. Still, my best guess is that misreading the meaning of my check-raise on the flop was the primary trigger for his aggression.

You're Already Doing It

Better players act according to how they read you. It follows that you can anticipate how they will act if you think about how they read you. What's more, you can manipulate how they will read you. You've been doing this all the time, perhaps without even knowing it. You do it every time you play deceptively. When you bluff, semi-bluff, or slowplay you are trying to mislead your opponents into reading you incorrectly in the hope that it will earn you more money. What I did in the hand above was simply another form of deception. If you look for others you will find them.

Acknowledgement: I would like to thank Sudhir Padmanabhan, with whom I discussed this hand. His insightful comments enabled me more clearly to present my thought processes in writing. (By the way, you too can benefit from his poker insights as he, along with myself and many others, is a regular participant on the forums at www.twoplustwo.com. This is *the* site for serious poker discussion on the net. See you there.)

Thinking About
What They're Thinking

Recently I came upon a note I had made a few years ago about a hand I played. Looking back on it, I found that it served to illustrate the important activity of thinking about what your opponents are thinking as you play. It was in a $15-$30 game in which most of the other players and I were playing "overs" (so it became $30-$60 when only overs players were in the pot). A short while earlier in that session, in which several opponents were occasional players who were not very familiar with my play, a hand had come up which would later influence my play in the hand in question. I had picked up pocket kings in the big blind. Several players were involved, and there had been a reraise by the time the action got to me. I capped the betting at four bets. I then check-raised on the flop, was called down by one player, and won the pot in a showdown.

About 20 minutes later I was dealt

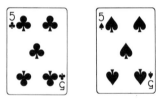

in the big blind. Two players limped, a third player raised, and three more players called the raise cold. (Believe it or not, this wasn't really that good a game. The preflop action in this and the previous hand had been something of an anomaly.) Believing that the limpers would probably call two more bets cold, I opted to make it three bets. I did this both in the hope of tying players onto the pot if I hit my set, and as a variation in my play to keep the determined readers off balance. Everyone called.

The flop came a disappointing:

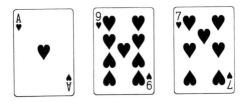

For a moment I considered betting out, trying to steal the pot by representing the strong hand (e.g., AA or AKs) that my preflop reraise had suggested. Though a case could be made for such a bet in some games, in my estimation, against this particular lineup, it was hopeless. There were many active opponents, some of whom were loose. Also, with that many players, there was a strong chance someone held at least an ace or a big heart. As this was an overs pot I couldn't check and call either. The pot contained about $320 (seven players in for three $15 bets preflop plus part of the small blind minus the house drop), but the bet on the flop would be $30, giving me only about 12-to-1 pot odds on a 23-to-1 shot, with one of my "outs" realistically giving me only a draw. In the next fraction of a second I realized however, that a check from me would look entirely consistent with how I had played when I check raised with the two kings out of the small blind. Maybe these guys would be "smart" enough to check along and avoid the check-raise that I appeared to be "planning" again. Then, maybe the free card I would get would be a lucky five. Though the five of hearts would give me only a draw, that was a draw I wanted to have. So I checked, and to my great satisfaction everyone did indeed check along. Now the turn came the

Scratch that plan about a five.

I knew that if I checked again two things would happen:

1. The other players would decide I didn't have anything, and
2. Someone would almost certainly bet — there were some fairly aggressive players in the game — forcing me to fold.

But all was not lost. In addition to their fear of a check-raise, everyone checking on the flop also supported the possibility that no one had much of a hand. If I bet now, it would still be consistent with the big starting hand I suspected my opponents thought I had. If everyone was weak, I might just be able to steal this pot with my little underpair. As this was an overs pot I had to bet $60 and so was getting only a little better than 5-to-1 pot odds. But the bigger bet would also be taken more seriously, and would likely shut out anyone who might otherwise think of calling with something less than an ace or a big heart. I bet and got just one caller, a slightly better than average player who I put on the king or queen of hearts. The river paired the six, thankfully with a diamond. I bet again, and my opponent thought a bit and folded, giving me the $440 pot.

At the time this seemed like quite a coup. Can I say for sure that it succeeded because I acted on the basis of what the other players were putting me on, and what they thought I was doing? No. Though I suspect that some of the players had been observant enough to relate my play to the earlier hand with the pocket kings, others may have been oblivious to such history. It may be that they just didn't have anything. I may, in fact, have been "bluffing with the best hand."

Nevertheless, by considering what they were thinking, I invested my money in a situation of maximum opportunity. If you invest repeatedly in the good situations instead of the bad ones, you will make a lot of money.

Out On the Edge

I walked into one of my regular cardroom haunts on a Friday afternoon. For some reason the usual crowd of $20-$40 hold 'em players had not materialized. I saw one game going three-handed. I knew the players, and also knew that while I welcomed two of them in a ring game, they were aggressive and would make for a challenging short-handed lineup. To make matters worse the third was a solid player who happened also to be experienced, and skilled at short-handed play. I had once played him heads-up for a brief time and had found him to be a tough, thinking player. Nevertheless, I enjoy short-handed play and felt I should still have an edge, though not of the magnitude I would normally like. As I expected the game to fill up before long anyway, I took a seat.

I quickly saw that the two normally loose, aggressive players had jacked up their usual levels of aggression by a couple of notches, and were deeply into an extreme "attack and counter" mode of play. Despite their usual over-aggressive styles and excessive bluffing these were thinking players. Their bets and raises were not indiscriminate. They bet aggressively, but were also capable of laying hands down. They were deceptive and had some mix in their play. Often they were functioning around the third level of thinking that Sklansky has described. (See the "Psychology of Poker" section in *The Theory of Poker*.) A player would bluff his opponent, who had a hand of equally little value, would suspect the buff and bluff-raise, then the first player, aware of the likelihood of the bluff-raise, would bluff-reraise.

In other words I realized that this game was even tougher and my edge even smaller than I had anticipated. I would often have opted to take a break until more players showed up. On this day, however, I was feeling good and saw it as an opportunity to sharpen my short-handed game.

Before describing the way one hand played out, I should mention that I do not present the hand to suggest that I had an easy time in this game. This just happened to be an especially interesting hand which I happened to remember, perhaps only because I won it. I would also like to point out that in an aggressive short-handed game such as this one, a play which might be correct at one moment, may be completely wrong just a short time later against the same opponent. Your image, your opponent's emotional state, and what he is thinking about the details of your play all change rapidly under these conditions. You must stay attuned to all of them to keep your edge.

I had been in the game for less than an hour. We were four-handed. I was in the big blind. The two players not in the blinds folded, and the small blind, whom I'll call Pierre, raised. He was one of the usually loose, aggressive players, and the better thinker of the two. I had suspected that he had stolen a couple of pots from me in previous hands. I knew he was capable of raising very loosely in this spot. At times he might do so with all but his weakest hands. I looked at my hand and saw:

I could have reraised. It would have been a reasonable option against some players, or against Pierre at a different time. I would have liked to send him the message that he would often be looking at three bets when he raised my blind. But I was not especially concerned about it at that point, as he had not so far been raising to excess in that spot anyway. More important was that at that time in the session I felt that my raising frequency was just beginning to approach a level at which Pierre would take my raises less seriously. This would damage my ability to bluff successfully, and invite even more resteal attempts from Pierre. With protecting my ability to bluff in mind, I simply called his raise.

Heads-up, we saw the flop come:

He bet. Should I fold, call, or raise? It was actually closer than it would look to many players used to playing only in ring games. In fact, readers without a lot of short-handed experience might understandably wonder how I could even consider anything other than a fold. Granted, under normal ring game conditions mucking here would be routine.

However, these were different circumstances. In short-handed play, especially when aggressive players are involved, bluffs and semi-bluffs come at a frequency that far exceeds that of typical ring game play. I knew that Pierre would almost certainly bet that flop regardless of his hand. If he had little or nothing, he would hope that I would fear a king and fold. With a stronger hand, he would bet in the hope that I would pay off. With a very strong hand he just might check, but might well bet even then, as he would know that I would find his check suspicious. Thus his bet did little to narrow down his hand, but since he would usually have little, yet still bet, there was a strong chance he was bluffing or semi-bluffing. Sure, he could have a hand like

or

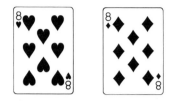

but those were no more likely than something like QT, A4, or 33. In fact, they were less likely. And he would just as readily bet with a hand like:

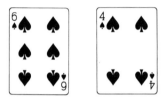

Against Pierre I had to consider that:

1. Queen-high might be the best hand on the flop.
2. If queen-high was not best, pairing either of my cards would give me a reasonable chance of winning.
3. I had a backdoor straight draw which could give me an open ended or gut shot draw on the turn.
4. I had the second nut backdoor flush draw.
5. If I hit either of these draws on the turn, the high likelihood that Pierre was bluffing would increase my chance of winning the pot on a semi-bluff as a resteal.

These factors dictated that I not fold. If I too often folded in a spot like this against Pierre, I would be giving up too much. Moreover, he would interpret my passivity as a license to steal from me every chance he got. No, folding was not the play here (though it could be at some other time). The choice was either raise or call.

Before I go on, let me note that having played similar hands before, I knew quickly on this flop what I was going to do. I did not need to spend time analyzing each option. Here I present a detailed analysis simply to show you the logic behind the play.

Returning to the hand, though a raise was not out of the question, it would border on being a pure bluff at that point in the hand. I had no outs that would give me a very strong hand, much less a sure winner on the turn. Moreover, the small flop bet would hardly give Pierre pause if he had any hope whatsoever of winning. He would be unimpressed by a raise on the cheap betting round, and would call, almost forcing me to bet again on the turn, extending my bluff over two rounds. This did not provide the kind of leverage I was looking for.

On the other hand, calling now on the chance of picking up either a pair, or one of my draws on the turn would give me the opportunity to semi-bluff when Pierre would take it more seriously and I would have outs that would likely win if they hit. (Cards that would accomplish this were any queen, jack, ten, nine, ace, or heart, for a total of 23 cards.) I knew as well that Pierre might opt not to bet again on the turn. So I might also have the option of taking a free card. I therefore called his bet on the flop.

The turn brought perhaps the best possible draw-creating card for me — the ten of hearts. I now had both a straight draw and a flush draw for 15 outs. (Of course there was some chance Pierre held the A♥ negating my flush outs). Pierre bet again and I raised. Pierre thought for several moments and called. His call could mean that he held a heart, a nine, a pair, or even just ace-high. The reason he might call with ace-high was that he knew that I realized he was a frequent bluffer, and therefore may have been aware that I might try to resteal from him with a semi-bluff. Well, I missed. The river was the K♠. The board now read:

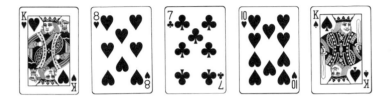

Pierre hesitated for a moment and bet.

Did he have a king? I doubted it. He had paused too long to think on the turn. Pierre was a player who would have called almost automatically with a king or better.[22] Moreover, with only trips now he would not be too likely to bet into me after I had so strongly represented a flush or straight . No, I put him not on a hand, but on a "move." His play was most consistent with a complete bust, a weak pair such as A7, or perhaps an ace-high hand with which he was trying to steal the pot using the paired king as a scare card. He probably hoped that I held a busted draw (as I did), and would not consider raising, or simply that the threat of trips would force me to fold a weaker hand. The problem for me was the possible one pair and ace-high hands he could hold. I could not call in the hope of winning with my queen because those hands represented a large portion of the hands he could have, especially in light of his having stayed with the hand till the river. With the high likelihood that he had very little, but just enough to beat me, it was clear that my best play was to *resteal* from him. I was sure my image with Pierre was at least fairly tight, and he would have a hard time not respecting a raise from me. He may have been skeptical that I held a big hand when I raised on the turn. But it *had* been consistent with a made hand, and a second raise now would go a long way toward erasing any

---

[22] This is why you should sometimes pretend to think even when you have nothing to think about.

skepticism. I did raise, he thought a couple of moments, and folded. I must stress again that given only slightly different circumstances a good case could have been made for a different action on my part at nearly any point in the hand. Had I not been slightly concerned about how Pierre was viewing my raises, for example, I might have reraised preflop. Had Pierre been a less aggressive, less frequent bluffer, I might have folded on the flop. The turn decision was routine, but calling instead of raising could have been an option under certain conditions. Finally, the raise on the river could easily have been wrong had I not been up against a player whose aggressiveness and bluffing frequency greatly reduced the chance that he held a hand with which he could (or would) call.

Poker decisions tend to be situational in nature. They depend very much on the specific circumstances of the hand. Never is this more true than in short-handed play. In short-handed games decisions are strongly influenced by how you think your opponents are seeing your play, how you want to affect their subsequent thoughts about it, broader image considerations, your opponents' emotional states, how you interpret subtle nonverbal cues, and more. Moreover, quick thinking is a plus as you are often faced with new, unanticipated options on successive betting rounds. Notice, for instance, in the hand I played, that I had not expected a bet from my opponent on the river and had to decide relatively quickly how to deal with it.

The combination of the call on the flop, the semi-bluff raise on the turn, and the bluff-raise on the river made this hand a bit "extreme," a hand played "out on the edge" relative to more typical hands. Such hands come up sometimes in short-handed play, more often than they do in ring games. They highlight the thought processes of poker and the situational nature of play. It follows that short-handed play can help sharpen your thinking for ring games where most of your play need not push the limits so hard. For more on playing short-handed see the essay, "Short-Handed Play: Don't Miss Out."

Considerations
in Two Blind
Stealing/Defense Situations

I write this essay with those of you in mind who are trying to move up to the middle limits. Relative to small games, in middle limit hold 'em ring games you will find yourself more often in blind stealing situations, playing hands out heads-up against a blind, or against the player who tried to steal your blind. Thus it is important to your success that you become fluent in negotiating these situations. For general starting hand guidelines both for stealing and defending blinds, I refer you to *Hold 'em Poker for Advanced Players: 21ˢᵗ Century Edition.* Its guidelines are correct and quite useable. With a little additional thought about the relative merits of high cards versus smaller suited cards in these spots, you should be off to a good start in knowing what hands to play. I would caution, as well, against trying to adopt guidelines which may differ dramatically from those in Sklansky and Malmuth's book. On the Internet, for example, I have seen some extremely liberal starting standards, derived from computer simulations, suggested for these situations. If you start defending your blind, for example, with hands such as Q4 and 73, as I have seen advocated, you *will* be throwing your money away.

Below I will detail two common situations, one involving a steal attempt, the other a defense of the big blind. For each situation, there is no one universally correct way to play. Rather, there are multiple factors you must consider in order to make your decision. Accordingly, though there is a most common play for each of these situations when viewed across all opponents, I will emphasize not what you should usually do, but what you should *think* about. I will provide a sampling of factors. By no means do the considerations I list exhaust all the possibilities. They are merely some highlights. However, not all of the elements I list in each situation will be important in a given real life hand against a specific opponent. Some might be. While at the same time factors completely different from those I mention, will often loom large.

This essay also points to the situational nature of poker. Because multiple variables interact in a hand, two situations which appear similar at first glance may, upon deeper analysis, point to completely different decisions. In fact, one of my purposes in writing this essay is to show how many considerations can be involved in what appear on the surface to be simple, routine poker situations. It is not enough simply to ask something like, "What hand did I make? Is it worth a bet?"

In fact, as I suspect even my partial list shows, there are often too many potentially relevant variables in a hand to account for all of them in the decision making process. At the same time, to ignore important factors will cost you money. A key, therefore, is to try to identify the elements of greater importance. Work on your ability to zero in on those factors.

I list the main categories under each situation in roughly the order you might think of them at the table. In reality though, it is an artificial separation, as the thought process actually tends to take place more as a whole.

Situation No. 1: You raise, hoping to steal the blinds from a late position. The big blind calls. The flop misses you. The big blind will now either bet or check. (On rare occasions he will simply muck his cards. It's a bad play on his part, and is a sign that your image is good.) First, suppose he bets. What should you do? You will often have to fold, but there are plenty of exceptions. A number of considerations must go into your decision:

1. The pot now contains about 5½ small bets. You will be getting 5½-to-1 on a call or 5½-to-2 (2¾-to-1) on a raise. These pot odds along with your estimated chance of stealing the pot, as well as implied odds if you have any significant outs, should inform your decision. (Of course depending on

how many outs you have, it might no longer be accurate to say you "missed.")

2. You must of course consider the cards. In what way did you miss the flop? Say you raise with

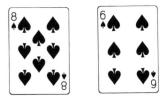

and the flop comes

Your situation there is different from when you raise with the same 8♠6♠ but the flop comes

or

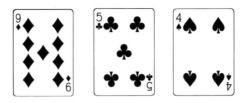

Some flops will give you a little leverage and allow you to play on, or to be more aggressive than you could be with other flops.

3. Similarly, the flop relates in some way to your opponent's hand. Its texture combined with what you know of your opponent's play, should give you some hint about how likely it was to have hit his hand. With what kinds of hands will he defend his big blind? Obviously, you should be less inclined to try to bluff-raise when the flop badly misses your hand, giving you effectively no outs, while your judgment tells you that it may well have hit your opponent's hand. This is part of the hand reading process at this point in the hand. You began reading your opponent's hand before the flop. Against an opponent who defends with a very wide range of hands, however, your read will of course be less precise.

4. You might now extend the hand reading process, with an emphasis on reading the player. The fundamental question is: What does his bet mean? Put in more general terms, how does your opponent play? Is he aggressive and/or deceptive? What about in this specific kind of situation? If he bets, does it very likely mean a hand, or does he do so liberally in this spot without having very much?

   If he is at all a thinking player, his action here will have been influenced in some part by how he currently sees *your* play. If he thinks you are easy to steal from, for example, the likelihood that his bet is a bluff goes up.

5. How is he likely to respond to each action you might take? This involves, perhaps even more clearly, the interaction between how he plays and how he currently sees your play. (Against some opponents, you need to go to the next level and think about how he thinks *you* view *his* play. In this essay however, I will leave it at the second level.) For example, if he is very aggressive and bluffs frequently, and also sees you as cautious and often willing to fold under pressure, he will more likely play back at you if you try to semi-bluff raise in this spot.

    Consider as well what will happen beyond the flop. If you call on the flop, is there a realistic chance he will check on the turn? If you raise, will he call and check to you on the turn? If you check along on the turn will he automatically bet into you on the river?

Now suppose he checks on the flop. This is actually the more common scenario. Though you will most often bet against typical opponents, the situation will occasionally dictate otherwise. You must again consider a number of factors:

1. Again, pot odds help guide your decision. The pot is laying you 4½-to-1 on a bet.

2. How your cards relate to the flop is again a consideration, but often less so than if he had bet. Though it depends on the opponent, on average you now have a better chance of stealing the pot with a bet. Should your opponent check-raise, however, the precise way in which you missed again becomes very important.

3. As above, beginning the postflop hand reading process, might this flop have hit your opponent's hand in some way? Considering what you know of the range of hands with which he will defend his big blind against your apparent steal

attempt, are you able to begin, at least roughly, to estimate the chance that he has a piece of this flop?

4. Just as when he bets, you must interpret his action. Does he tend to play straight forwardly, or is he a frequent check-raiser in this spot? Is he capable of a check-raise bluff, or semi-bluff? Is he a habitual slowplayer? Does he wait until the turn to play his stronger hands? Is he a passive player who will simply give you free cards until he makes something?

   Consider how his view of your play may have influenced his action. Has he observed that you invariably bet when checked to in this spot? Does he think you are easy to run over?

   His check does provide you with valuable information. Though you may have no outs, and the flop may be one that would seem more likely to have hit your opponent, he did check. Often that simply means he has nothing and is prepared to give up the pot.[23] While he may be planning to raise or slowplay a strong hand, a check on his part is nevertheless the only action consistent with an unwillingness to contest the pot.

5. How is he likely to respond if you bet versus checking along? (Remember, you will not often check, but there are exceptions.) Here again, how he plays, combined with how he sees your play will strongly influence his action. If he believes, for instance, that you rarely bet without a hand, and that you are difficult to steal from, then he is less likely to check-raise as a bluff or semi-bluff. Thus, you may have more reason to bluff bet. Then if he does check-raise, you can assume he more likely has a real hand. Do you estimate that he will fold to your bet often enough (about 18 percent of the

---

[23] This is obviously less true against players who will always check to the raiser in this situation.

time, given the size of the pot) to make a pure bluff profitable? (He does not have to fold as often for a semi-bluff to show a long term profit.) If you check, how will the way he sees your play influence his action on the turn with a weak hand versus a strong one? If you bet and he calls, will he likely check to you on the turn? If you then take a free card will he usually take the opportunity to bluff into you on the river?

Situation No. 2: You defend your big blind with a call against a likely steal raise from a late position player. The flop misses you. Your decision now is between checking and betting. If you are going to continue with the hand, rather than checking and folding, then you must decide between checking and calling, check-raising, and betting out.

1. The pot is laying you about 4½-to-1 on a bet. It will lay you 5½-to-1 on a call or 5½-to-2 on a check-raise if you check and your opponent bets. (It becomes 6½-to-4 if you think he will almost automatically call your check-raise, but then may fold to a subsequent bet on the turn.) These pot odds will figure into any decision. Notice, for instance, that if you are considering attempting to steal the pot, the risk-reward ratio for betting is better than that for check-raising. That does not necessarily mean you should bet instead of check-raising, but it is an important consideration when thinking about the expectation of one approach versus the other.

2. As before, what you do will be influenced by the nature of how the flop relates to your hole cards, despite your having "missed." Some flops will give you semi-bluffing possibilities, while some won't. Some may allow for a call if you check and your opponent bets. (For example, this will be the case some of the times when you have overcards.) Others will point toward a fold.

3. Note as well the texture of the flop combined with what you know of your opponent's starting hand requirements for raising your blind from a steal position. Analogous to your having considered the flop as it related to the possible hands of the blind defender, this is central to beginning the postflop hand reading process. If your opponent is very liberal in his blind stealing attempts you may have to settle for a read that is more general, more a rough estimate of the chance he has a piece of the flop. (But note that such a player is less likely to have a hand when the flop comes with high cards.)

4. How is he likely to respond to a bet versus a check? As before, how he plays may be heavily dependent on how he sees your play. What is your current image with this player? If you check-raise, how is he likely to respond to that? Will he almost automatically call? How might he then respond to a bet on the turn? Will he likely call on the flop with overcards? Will he call all the way with a small pair? How about ace-high?

While you cannot expect to always identify and assess every important consideration in these and other common poker situations, there is a way to improve your effectiveness in that regard. Simply think about such scenarios away from the table. Analyze your play in specific situations against one of your regular opponents who is challenging to play against. Develop a profile of his play, how you think he views your play, and how he seems to play against you as a consequence. Try as well to identify any flaws in his play. You will then be in a position to play more effectively against him.

Easing the Transition
to the Middle Limits: Part I

Most serious poker players would like to play at the highest limit that their bankroll will allow, and at which they can still achieve a good hourly rate in relation to the limit. No doubt many readers of this book are playing in lower limit games with the hope of moving up to the middle limits. To help increase your chance of success, I am going to provide some strategy tips that should help as you venture into bigger games. (I am not discussing bankroll requirements here, a subject of vital importance as you move up. This is covered well elsewhere in books such as Mason Malmuth's *Gambling Theory and Other Topics*.) Bear in mind that these are only helpful tips; the real key to success is a well rounded set of poker skills. This can be acquired through study and experience. Nevertheless, as you move up you will encounter opponents who play differently, on the whole more skillfully, than what you are used to. These tips should help ease your adjustment to these players. In Part II I will discuss three more general concepts. Here I offer three strategy tips:

1. **Take advantage of players' aggression.** As soon as you move up, you will notice that your opponents will tend to play more aggressively than what you have likely become used to in smaller games. They will try to steal from you more often, and will keep the pressure on with bets and raises, forcing you into more difficult decisions. Moreover, you will encounter this in what will more often be heads-up or three-handed pots. In general, this is indicative of the improvement in play which comes with increasing limits (see below). You must think about how to deal with these more aggressive players. Over time you will need to identify the individual characteristics — apart from the common trait of

aggressiveness — of your opponents' play so that you can zero in on and take advantage of their weaknesses. You will also need to develop your ability to think and make adjustments quickly in the heat of play. Short of such complete strategy development and execution, there are a couple of simple strategic ideas which can help you as you begin adjusting to skilled aggressive players.

First, notice that the more consistently aggressive a player is, the more relentless his bets and raises, the more often he is betting without a hand. In other words a player who is skilled, but very consistently aggressive is surprisingly similar to a habitual bluffer. Thus, you can play such a player something like you would a habitual bluffer — inducing bluffs by checking and calling more often. You do this some of the time with mediocre hands, such as middle pair, to let the aggressive player bluff off his money in situations where his actions would be less profitable for you if you bet. That is, if you bet he might simply fold many hands, and would raise with others. If he approaches being a habitual bluffer, you would generally profit less from either of these actions than from his betting after you check.

Note, however, that with such a marginal hand as middle pair you must read your opponent well. If his hand selection is fairly tight there will often be a reasonable chance that he does indeed hold top pair or better. You do not simply call him down automatically. It's a delicate decision. One advantage however of this check-call approach for the player just moving up to a higher limit game is that it allows you to avoid the tricky decisions that arise from being raised.

You can sometimes follow this same strategy with fairly good hands (or even very good hands) such as top pair with a good kicker. Here you might say you are mainly inducing your opponent *not to fold*. Compared to those times when you choose this tactic with something like middle pair, you would not be faced with as difficult a decision if he were to raise. Your main concern here is that he not fold, that he keep putting bets in the pot with a hand far inferior to yours. In other words, you have a hand which you would normally like to bet for value. But here, against an unusually aggressive opponent, you will often do better to focus on making sure he doesn't fold, and that he puts in a bet on every round. (This play works better when your top pair is high so he is not apt to have overcards. See *Hold 'em Poker for Advanced Players: 21st Century Edition* for more discussion.)

Remember, however, that we are talking about fairly skilled opponents. Therefore, you cannot get away with following only this strategy all the time. You must vary your play enough that your opponents cannot easily be sure what you are up to. Sometimes you check and call with top pair, sometimes you bet it, sometimes you check-raise. The decision is based on situational variables (or sometimes even pure randomness). My point here is simply that as you begin to play in these tougher games, using the check-call approach a little more often can ease the transition, because it is rather easy to apply without making serious errors. The same cannot be said of an approach which pushes the envelope of aggression. I would recommend that a player who is just moving up, but who lacks sufficient confidence in his skills vis-à-vis those of his new opponents, use this check-call approach against aggressive players somewhat more than is optimal, until he has mapped out more complete strategies based on increased familiarity with these opponents. Even for the expert, it remains an important element in his repertoire.

2. **Counter and take advantage of their awareness and thinking.** As you move up in limits, a key characteristic which will separate your new opponents from those you faced in the lower limits is that they will be thinking more effectively. Specifically, more of your opponents will be thinking about what hand you have, and how to play against you. You thus have the opportunity to take advantage of what they're thinking about your play. Indeed, as you deal with

more and more tough opponents you *must* take advantage of it if you are to beat the game for more than a minimal amount.

There is one type of opponent, common at these limits, who is especially vulnerable to the player who can deduce what he's thinking and take advantage of it. This player focuses much of his energy on characterizing players' styles and reading hands. That is one of his main strengths, but he does so in a very rigid way. Once he has decided how you play, you have to show him something radically different to make him change his mind. Similarly, once he puts you on a hand, he is so confident in his read that he has trouble revising it.

This description could of course apply to players who otherwise vary their play in many different ways. Here's an informal observation to help you identify players with this trait. I would note that it seems many of these good, but rigid readers are too loose and fairly aggressive preflop. Their play after the flop tends to be relatively skillful, but is often a bit over aggressive, with an excessively high bluffing frequency. I think these often are self taught players who have a good feel for the game, but whose main weakness is simply that of playing a little too loose-aggressively. There seems to be some correlation between these traits and the "rigid reading" trait. Still, bear in mind that this describes only one type of opponent who may have the trait under discussion. Certainly you will encounter this rigid reading and typing tendency in other kinds of players. (For an example of a hand played against such a player see the essay, "Countering a Good Reader.")

So how can you take advantage of this player's thinking? Simply, you play your hand a little more deceptively. Make him think you have something other than your actual hand. Here's a simple example.[24] Say you open for a raise on the button with:

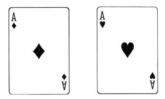

The big blind, who happens to fit the description of the aggressive, rigid reader, reraises you. Rather than raise again, which could be the right play against some unthinking players in a low limit "no fold 'em" game, for example, you should consider just calling. By just calling you avoid giving your hand away to a player who would understand and adapt to the meaning of another bet. You are then often in a position to extract on later streets more than what you gave up preflop. I should also point out that some of these rigid readers will tend to assume that a tight player plays very straight forwardly. Therefore when you just call, not only do you avoid giving this player an indication that you have a hand like A♦A♥ or K♦K♥, but he may read your call to mean quite clearly that you *don't* have such a hand. The last time I made this play, I put my opponent on a big pair of his own and we went four bets on a ragged flop before it dawned on him that I might just have him beat.[25] Of course he called me down the rest of the way.

There are plenty of other ways to inject an element of deception into your game both before and after the flop. Some are more complex and sophisticated than the simple

---

[24] Note that this play is fairly well known and works against many other kinds of players too.

[25] Waiting until the turn to raise is of course another reasonable way to play this hand.

example I have provided. If you think enough about the game, you'll be able to devise other plays. For example, if you've read *Hold 'em Poker for Advanced Players: 21st Century Edition*, you may recall that Sklansky and Malmuth recommend some ways of varying your play before the flop. Though the plays they suggest have a number of benefits against other kinds of opponents as well, they are part of the arsenal that you must use to defeat the strong but rigid reader.[26]

Keep in mind that your goal is to get the strong reader to put you on the wrong hand. Frequently you accomplish this through a bit more, or a bit less aggression, at some point in the hand, than would normally be expected on the basis of hand strength alone.[27]

Be aware that against unthinking opponents you should use such plays very infrequently. They are to be reserved primarily for use against those players whose reading skills are strong enough that conventional play has lost much of it's expected value. You reestablish EV through deception designed to foil their reads such that they either pay you off,

---

[26] There are many otherwise decent players who don't add this mix to their play. They make only the standard plays, assuming they can more or less ignore such "deception plays," since they're not the plays you're supposed to make most of the time anyway. While they may be right in some soft games, full of unthinking players, they are wrong when it comes to games containing players who think, observe, and adapt. You should be thankful that so many players shun these plays. That they are not seen terribly often at the poker tables makes them all the more effective when you do use them.

[27] Sometimes, however, you do it by playing straight forwardly when your opponent would expect you to play more "deceptively" with the hand you hold.

or concede the pot to you when they would not otherwise have done so.

Another part of adding deception to your game is generally varying your play more. Varying your play is hardly necessary in typical small limit games in which most players play without thinking very incisively. As you move up however, the average skill level of your opponents will increase, as will their average level of awareness. There will frequently be enough players in your games, with enough awareness and the skills to make use of it, that you must play a bit more deceptively in general. Therefore, in addition to the targeting of specific players for deception, you should aim consistently to vary your play a little more than you would in a typical small limit game. Remember though that you should typically make the play that maximizes your expectation on that hand. The more unusual plays must still be the exception rather than the rule. Make them too often and you'll be giving up profits.

3. **Tighten up during your period of adjustment.** Many players do this naturally out of fear of larger losses when they move up. Still, it's important enough that I want to stress it. By tightening up your starting requirements you will generally reduce your fluctuations, as well as your exposure to difficult decisions. By tightening up a bit after the flop as well, you will further reduce your fluctuations. Your postflop tightening, by which I mean folding a bit more when you would normally call or raise, should mainly center around marginal, small edge situations. Such tightening theoretically costs a little in hourly rate, but most players who are trying to get comfortable at a higher limit are glad to accept this in exchange for less volatility, and more frequent wins. Moreover, the reality is that it will often enable the less than super-expert player to achieve a *better* hourly rate than he would in the pursuit of smaller edges that, for him, are not really there. Do not, however, get carried away with this idea,

particularly the postflop part. If you start throwing away hands after the flop that actually have good chances of winning, just because you run into a little resistance, you'll give up too much.

As an example of tightening preflop, if the worst offsuit hands you normally play in an early position are hands like

and

you might eliminate them and play only AK and AQ, unless the game is soft. As an example of postflop tightening, you might pass on an opportunity to raise a bettor on the flop when you hold second pair. Usually you must fold in this spot anyway. Of the occasions when such a raise is correct, a fair percentage are only very marginally so. They can, in fact, turn into losing plays if you have not read the opponent's hand well and do not play excellently for the rest of the hand. Thus, you will give up little, and may well increase your profits by passing on almost all such raising opportunities (folding instead) during an initial adjustment period at your new, higher limit. I leave it to the reader to develop further examples of such tightening. Once you feel you have adjusted to the limit, you can minimize any slightly weak-tight spots in your game that may have resulted by beginning to push smaller edges as your ability allows.[28]

---

[28] It is important to appreciate how easy it is to cross the line attempting to push small edges, and begin to play in what are actually losing situations. The better a player you are the more edges you'll be able to find, many of them quite small, but there is a limit to this for every player. Moving past that limit into losing territory is a common, seductive, and very costly mistake.

Easing the Transition
to the Middle Limits: Part II

In Part One of this two part essay, I provided three strategy tips intended to help players make a more comfortable transition from the smaller limits to the middle limits. Here in Part II, I touch on three broader ideas, not specifically strategic in nature, that should help as well with this move up.

1. **Put more emphasis on game selection.** When you play in small limit games, game selection is frequently not terribly important. Of course, you might reasonably elect not to play in an unusual $3-$6 game which just happens to contain all the best $3-$6 players in town, or a $6-$12 game in which several good players from higher limit games are playing while they wait for seats in their regular games, but those are exceptions. Most often there are several players in a small limit game who are weak enough that it is reasonable to go ahead and play. This is less often the case in middle limit games. Though at the time of this writing there are areas of the country said to have consistently soft middle limit games, in areas where such limits have been in place for a long time it is not rare to find a game containing several fairly good players, and no really weak players. If you are not fairly experienced and one of the best players in the game yourself, such a game may be best avoided. Even if you think you are as good as most of the players in the game, if you see no one who is considerably less skilled than you, you might only expect a marginal hourly rate. Then you are producing little more than fluctuations, and are less likely to win in a given session. So, to the extent possible in your area, be especially picky about what games you sit down in during your initial period of adjustment.

2. **Analyze your play against specific opponents.** In the smaller games, the overall level of play is bad enough that you can survive and perhaps do fairly well, spending only a modest amount of time analyzing the play of specific opponents. This is not always true in the middle limits. There you will encounter more players who do not so easily give their money away. Among them will be some who lose only a little, and whose style of play can create real problems for a better player who hasn't looked closely at what they are doing. Then of course there are the tough, winning players whose play you will have to understand if you are not to give them your money.

When dealing with an opponent who gives you problems, you must think systematically about that person's play and develop effective counter-strategies. You can do this by keeping records and dissecting hands you've played against that person. Analyze them with an eye toward identifying any habitual patterns in his play, how well he plays, how he seems to view your play, and what kinds of mistakes you've made against him. You should then be in a position to identify more effective strategic approaches to dealing with this player.

Some opponents, though dangerous, lack the proper balance and mix in their play. They overemphasize certain tactics. Against them it is not difficult to develop well defined strategies which you can apply consistently and with great effect. In dealing with more skilled opponents the emphasis is more on determining at what level they are thinking (e.g., is he thinking only about what I have or is he thinking about what I think he has, or beyond?) and staying a step ahead of them. You play more of a cat and mouse game, trying to make them "zig when they should zag."

3. **Learn to play short-handed.** Unless you are already quite comfortable with short-handed play, this advice is really for after you have become more accustomed to the middle limits.

I offer it because you will find that middle limit games tend to become short-handed more often than small limit games. This is simply because there are fewer players available to keep them full. Therefore, if you consistently shun short-handed play you will not only play fewer hours in the middle limits, but you will miss some of the more profitable opportunities available in poker. So while I do *not* suggest that you indiscriminately jump into a lot of short-handed games while you are cutting your teeth in the middle limits, I do recommend, as you progress and become more comfortable at these limits, that you make the effort to learn about, and then try your hand at more and more short-handed poker. You may even find that it becomes a favorite part of your poker play.

Conclusion

I have provided only a few ideas which should help players moving up the limits. Many more could be mentioned, but such ideas can never be more than supplements to what is really needed for success at escalating limits — a solid understanding of the game as a whole. If you have that, then you should not find winning in the middle limits to be terribly difficult. Yes, the game will be a little tougher than at the small limits, but not as much as you might expect, especially if you exercise a little game selection. With the right set of skills you may find your move up to be a pleasant surprise.

Multiple Changing Images

Students of poker theory should be thoroughly familiar with the ideas about "image" that have often appeared in the poker literature. In various articles, Mike Caro has argued that a loose, wild, playful image is best, as it makes money by encouraging opponents merely to increase their most common error, calling too much. This allows you to get more value for your good hands. In articles and essays such as the one titled "Appropriate Image" in *Poker Essays*, Mason Malmuth has countered that in some games, notably hold 'em and seven-card stud, there is more to be gained from an image which enables you to steal the pot a bit more often than from an image that elicits calls. He therefore advocates a tight but aggressive image for these games. David Sklansky added to the discussion with an essay titled simply, "Image" in *Getting the Best of It,* in which he describes the value of a tight, timid image, and points out the utility of taking advantage of whatever image has been created for you by the cards you've been getting during a session.

In the loose image/tight image debate, I come down on the tight side, at least when it comes to hold 'em. If you are going to nurture one image, I think tight is the way to go. It's difficult to gain as many extra bets on your good hands via a loose image as you can pick up by stealing an occasional pot that would otherwise not be yours. This is especially true against somewhat skilled opponents. It is true, however, that you cannot avoid your image being affected by the cards you've been getting and the ways in which hands have played out. Thus, you must adjust to it.

Many Opponents, Many Images

My purpose here is not to pursue this debate any further. Rather, I would simply like to add one additional element to the discussion of image: Note that the discussions of image have generally revolved around what might be termed your "general" image, or how your opponents on average are seeing your play. As Sklansky points out, this image does vary over time as a function of the cards you receive. What I would like to add is that *at any given time your image may be markedly different in the perceptions of different opponents.* Depending on how you have played hands against *specific opponents*, some may see you as tight, conservative, and rarely bluffing, while at the same time others view you as an habitual bluffer. Some may view you as someone easy to run over, while others fear your aggression.

These multiple images are subject to change frequently as a result of subsequent hands played against these opponents. Opponents with at least a little sophistication adjust to how they believe you are playing. If they subsequently believe you have changed how you are playing, they readjust. Since random variations in the cards and opponent-specific strategic considerations will cause you to play differently against different opponents, those opponents will view your play differently and make correspondingly different adjustments.

This coexistence of multiple images is less likely to occur, or will be less pronounced, in games containing more observant opponents. Such opponents will watch not only how you play against them, but against others as well. They will therefore perceive more accurately how you are playing in general, and in varying circumstances. Nevertheless, in most games there will be some players who do not perceive you as others do. Multiple images will also be less a factor against more sophisticated players who have some ability to see *through* image and perceive the reality of how you play.

Multiple images are thus most likely to be a factor in games containing less observant, less sophisticated players. They will also occur when new players enter the game. The new players will start out with whatever baseline image they have of you, while those who have been playing against you for a while will have been affected in their views of you by hands you have played in the session so far. For example, you might generally have a conservative, non-bluffing sort of image. But, if you have been caught bluffing a few times during a session, the opponents who have witnessed this may see you, at least temporarily, as likely to bluff. At the same time, players who have just joined the game, and so were not privy to your failed steal attempts, will see you as they usually do (if they know you), as a non-bluffer. You may then be able to steal relatively easily from some opponents, while simultaneously needing to concentrate only on betting for value against others. (This of course is separate from other considerations, such as opponent playing tendencies, that go into such decisions.)

Thus, to take full advantage of image you must keep track not only of what you have conveyed generally to the table as a whole, but also of your image in the eyes of individual players. The two may be quite different.

Examples of the Use of Multiple Images

The idea of multiple images can apply to innumerable situations in poker. One of the easiest to understand, however, is how it impacts your ability to bluff, or bet for value. I will therefore present two examples in this area.

First consider this simple situation. You are playing against relatively unobservant opponents. A short while ago against opponent A you got caught bluffing. After that, against opponent B, you twice won pots showing down very strong hands. You may now need to concentrate on betting for value, and not attempting to bluff opponent A. At the same time, your chance of successfully stealing against opponent B has gone up.

Now here's a real world, slightly more complex example. Not long ago, during a short handed $20-$40 hold 'em game, I recognized that a particular opponent probably saw me as habitually bluffing, or perhaps as on tilt. The other players knew me well enough to know that the possibility I was on tilt was remote (to say the least), and probably hadn't noticed anything remarkable about my play at the time. Against this one player however, there had been about three hands in close succession in which I raised or reraised preflop, then semi-bluffed on the flop and turn, missed my draw, and bluffed again or just gave up on the end.

I knew a couple of things about this opponent. First, I knew that he was not very familiar with my play. Second, in the two or three times I had played with him I had noticed that he very much liked to let others bet his hand for him. This undoubtedly worked reasonably well for him as he had a generally tight, cautious image and probably experienced lots of players trying to run over him. I began to sense that he overdid this, and was playing as if he suspected others of trying to bluff against him more often than they actually were. (Yes, he happened to have won against me in this manner in the hands described, but that does not mean my play in those hands was incorrect or that his was correct. In a short handed game, the difference between a semi-bluff and a bet for value with an ace high hand, for example, can become quite blurry.) If I was right, if he was especially prone to suspect others of bluffing, then I reasoned that after catching me in about three (semi) bluffs over a short period, he should certainly be expecting more bluffs from me. He might even assume I was on tilt. (Why else would I try to buff three times in a row?) Moreover, I was sure that he was the *only* player at the table who saw me this way at that time. This was because it was he against whom I had tried my unsuccessful bluffs, while the other players had not been observing very intently

Just a few minutes later I picked up

in the small blind. He open-raised on the button. I reraised. I did so, aware that he may have seen me as simply playing back wildly with a mediocre hand. The two of us saw the flop which came:

I bet, again knowing that he would believe there was no reason to assume I had a pair, much less an ace. True to form, he called. At that point, because of how I believed he viewed me, I felt that *he* could have any pair or a draw. The turn was a 5. Again, I bet and he called. The river was a K, a bad card for me. However, it did not change the fact that he was going to call me with any pair, or maybe even with queen-high. Also, I did not think this player would bluff or bet anything less than a king if I checked. So I bet again, and he again called. I turned over my Q♥Q♦, and he mucked his hand.

The point of the example above is to show how keeping track of the image you have in the minds of individual players earn you extra money at the table. In the hand I played I was able to collect an extra bet by betting my queens for value despite the two overcards on board. I would most likely have checked in the same spot against any other player in the game that day. I would have figured them to be less likely to call with a hand I could beat, though I might have induced a bluff with my check.

So keep track of your image and how it changes on both general and player-specific levels. That way you will know more precisely what your opponents are thinking as you play against them; for they are not really playing against you, but rather against your multiple, changing images.

Strategic
Thinking in Hold 'em
Afterthought

While the section just concluded contains a number of specific plays which some readers might find interesting, I hope thoughtful readers come away as well with useful concepts and perhaps even new ways of thinking about strategy during play. Much of the material focused on reading opponents' hands and thoughts. In my view these areas of play are a large part of what makes poker interesting. Moreover, they become increasingly important as you move up the limits; for they are at the center of the strategic interaction between skilled players. If you understand card play in some detail, and have a grasp of basic odds, becoming proficient in these two kinds of reading will boost your results substantially. I hope this section helped a bit in that regard.

Part Four

Poker and Emotion

Poker and Emotion

Introduction

In my opinion the topic of this section has traditionally been a bit under emphasized in the poker literature. While it is true that fundamentally correct play is the primary ingredient in one's poker success, I cannot overemphasize the extent to which countless competent players damage or destroy their results by acting on emotion during play. Now, as a psychologist I would never suggest that you ignore or deny feelings. Psychotherapists expend a great deal of energy helping patients to recognize and verbalize their feelings. Nevertheless, if you *act* on feelings like frustration, anger, or helplessness at the poker table, you will pay for it. Here are some ideas to help you avoid this. For many of you, setting things straight in this area may prove to be the single most important factor in turning your results around.

I do not attempt here to look as deeply as possible at the problem of emotion in poker. As suggested in some of the essays, looked at from some of the major psychological points of view, these struggles have roots deep in the unconscious, largely untouchable outside the walls of a skilled therapist's office. Nevertheless, for those whose problems with tilt are not too serious, the ideas provided can definitely help.

How Am I
Doing? *Who Cares?*
Moving Beyond
Excess Focus on Fluctuations

Poker is a double edged sword. If you play well you will win in the long run. During that long run however, you cannot avoid the fluctuations that come with the game. You must accept inevitable losses if you are to play and win. Ironically, one could even argue that, as a winning player, you should *welcome* your losses; for they reflect the balance of luck and skill which must be present to allow weaker players to win often enough for the games to thrive. As one friend of mine says, "Fluctuations are your friend," but few players are able to feel very welcoming of their downswings, and most make too much of their upswings. Moreover, the vast majority of players are constantly and intensely focused on how they are doing *right now*. This is their central concern as they play. This leads them to reach faulty conclusions about themselves, and their play. What they fail to appreciate is that when they focus on their fluctuations in assessing how they are playing, they are wasting time with the wrong data instead of with what matters.

"I've Been Winning.
Would You Like Lessons?"

The faulty conclusions I am referring to involve a player's responding to his short term results in isolation, as if they reflect his skill level (or even his worth as a person!). We've all seen the mediocre or poor player who happens to run hot for a while and takes it to mean that he's playing exceptionally well. Perhaps he

205

just talks about his "great play," boasting of some incredible hourly rate, or maybe he moves up to a higher limit. Of course either way he eventually loses back all his winnings as his results, given more time, do reflect his skill level. To make matters worse, this player's downswing is liable to be magnified by what the upswing does to his play. For a player who does not engage in regular self examination concerning his play — most players — running well will reinforce his existing errors. That is, his winning despite poor play serves as a reward for his errors. This is so as long as he makes the mistake of assuming that his winning means he is playing well, and that he can continue winning by playing in the same way.

The conclusion reached here can be dangerously convincing for a player who lacks sufficient knowledge of gambling theory and probability. For to some extent he *is* winning because of how he is playing. For example, he may play far too many hands, but if he happens to have a sustained run of good luck with his substandard hands they will win him a lot of money — in the short term. Although he is costing himself money every time he plays a substandard hand, the cost will not be apparent to him during his lucky streak. Only in the long run is it guaranteed to manifest itself. In fact, when he has such a winning streak he can accurately say, "I never could have won as much during this recent period had I not played all those hands." Thus he is likely to continue to play the same hands in the future, eventually wondering why he has lost so much when he was doing so well for a time. At the center of this player's plight is his focus on a red herring — his short term fluctuations. It leads him to reach the wrong conclusion about his play.

While less knowledgeable players are the most likely to form this faulty conclusion, those more educated in the game are not above similarly flawed thinking. It is common for a good player who has an unusually good winning streak to begin, perhaps just slightly, to expect that he will continue to win with ease. Again, he is fixed on the wrong data. Consequently he may begin subtly to overplay some hands, to draw a bit thin, to play a few hands that his better judgement would say to fold. It may only be well after his good luck has turned around that he recognizes where he is playing badly. By that time it has cost him substantially, but a good player who persists at improving his game will eventually learn to avoid this trap. With experience he can learn to maintain proper play whatever his short term results have been.

Negative fluctuations can lead to the opposite conclusion. As a result of an unavoidable losing streak a good player may conclude that he is not very skilled after all. Because he is running badly, he finds that no matter what he does he simply can't win. Eventually this experience can engender a feeling of helplessness which erodes his usual sense of confidence in his abilities. He concludes that maybe he never really knew how to play, maybe he's been doing lots of things wrong without realizing it. Here again, if he has in fact been playing well, the error is one of equating his skill level with his short term results. The consequence may be a deterioration in his play as emotion, rather than reason, begins to dominate his decisions.

Just as winning and losing streaks can trigger faulty conclusions, swings within a session can do the same. Here the conclusion is often less well structured. A player does not necessarily think, "I'm winning a lot right now, so I must be an excellent player." Rather he just feels good, as evidenced by his visibly cheery mood or increased talkativeness. Still, some players do seem to act as though an upswing is simply a well deserved reflection of their superior play. It is fascinating to see a really bad player adopt an air of smug superiority after catching a lot of good cards and holding over his opponents for a while.

On the other hand, a downswing can easily bring down a player's mood. This phenomenon is so common, in fact, that it seems there is scarcely a player immune to it. It is one of the chief triggers of going "on tilt," but it is an irrational reaction which will occur less often, and with less intensity, if a player is not distracted by the wrong data.

What are the right data? They are the specifics of his play. By focusing on why he has played hands in specific ways, and analyzing the correctness of his play, independent of any short term results, he will put himself in a position to reach correct conclusions about how he is playing.

Why is Everyone so Distracted?

The question then is why so many players focus unproductively on their short term fluctuations. I believe I can provide at least a partial answer. The degree to which a player is likely to attend to short term swings, and therefore form the faulty conclusions described, appears to be largely a function of four factors. (Certainly there are other elements at work as well, but these four are key.)

1. **The wrong goal.** The first involves the basic goal a player has in mind when he sits down to play. As strange as it may sound, most players are too focused on winning. It is far more productive to make correct play your goal and let winning take care of itself. Yet few players seem truly to appreciate this. Most are drawn misguidedly to be concerned with their short term monetary results. When they win they become self satisfied and assume they're doing everything right, and when they lose they waste time cursing their bad beats, as if they've been singled out to have uniquely bad luck. I cannot overstate how counterproductive these responses are.

    This focus on the wrong goal is nearly always involved in reaching the erroneous conclusions about one's skill level that I have described. If you are a serious player you can do yourself a favor by learning enough poker theory to determine how well you are playing by analyzing your play itself rather than concerning yourself with your recent fluctuations. This analysis, along with your hourly rate (over enough hours to be meaningful), will put you in a position to assess accurately how you are playing.

Concern with the wrong goal is quite natural in poker. You sit down to play a game; in games you try to win. Yet in poker, as in some other games, over-concern with winning rather than simply trying to play well, can hurt your end result.

Of course there are plenty of winning players who maintain this focus which I am saying is wrong. Many winning players, in fact, would say that they have never even considered the possibility of a goal other than simply winning. I believe that the majority of the players who win the most over the long run unwittingly adopt the correct focus much of the time. Yes, they want to win, but to some extent they put that out of their minds, and much of the time concentrate more on correct play.

2. **Inadequate knowledge.** Merely knowing the correct focus is not enough. A player must be able to do something productive with the data he examines. When he cannot, it is because of the second factor: The lack of sufficient knowledge of poker theory. Without this knowledge a player's focus moves inevitably back to what he sees most clearly, his fluctuations.

3. **Lack of knowledge of probability.** One component of the second factor is important enough to be mentioned separately. This factor is the knowledge of probability as it relates to gambling theory in general, and poker in particular. If a player does not have an accurate appreciation for the random nature of the fluctuations experienced in poker, he will begin incorrectly to attribute meaning to them. He will say, "Look, I've won so much lately I must be the best player around." This is not unlike the player who decides that it means something that he has often won when he sits in a certain seat, or wears a certain shirt. The player's results, though distributed randomly, have, for some period, fallen within what looks to him like a nonrandom pattern which he

can see in *retrospect*. He believes this is meaningful. He cannot appreciate that within a random distribution, patterns of all sorts will eventually appear.

4. **Problems with self-esteem.** Difficulty with self-esteem may lead a player to form certain self-deceptions. It is not my intent here to address the topic of self-esteem, a subject which the interested reader can explore in the psychological literature. However, coming from a background in clinical psychology, I feel compelled to share some simple observations which should be of interest to players who are affected adversely by their monetary swings.

    To posit a rough correlation, I would say that to the degree that one has a problem with self-esteem, one's behaviors will reflect that problem, either in demonstrating the need to protect self-esteem, or in betraying its fragility. What this means for a poker player is that any problem he has with self-esteem may influence his actions, thoughts, or feelings during (or about) his play. This can extend to numerous areas of the game. With regard to the kinds of flawed thinking I have described here, note that a player who has had a winning streak may seize the opportunity to conclude that he is a great player. Conversely, a good player who has been losing may react so self critically that he concludes that he really can't play. A player may have similar reactions to monetary swings within a single session. For instance, the intensity of the depressing effect of a downswing, described above, seems closely connected to matters of self-esteem.[29]

---

[29] Before the reader discounts this factor as one applying only to a few individuals with unfortunate emotional problems, let me point out that my background in clinical psychology removed for me any doubt that difficulties with self-esteem are so common in our society that they approach being universal. For many these difficulties are relatively minor, but still exert some influence over their behavior.

In many instances, this emotional factor may actually be the origin of the first factor described above. A player may be too narrowly focused on winning because he needs to win to bolster his self-esteem. Paradoxically, his need to win will adversely impact his play, making him more likely to lose.

If you have a minor problem in this area, you may be able consciously to train yourself to separate your attitude about your short term results from your self-esteem, thereby keeping the latter from affecting your decisions. One effective way of doing this is to tie your self-esteem to the quality of your play rather than your results. You consciously try to feel good about good decisions during play rather than monetary outcome. Ideally (and admittedly this may be just an ideal for many players) you should be able to feel quite good about yourself after a session in which you lost badly, because you know you played consistently well that session. This is similar to an idea Sklansky discusses in his essay, "Will Power" in *Poker, Gaming, & Life*. If you have a more significant problem with self-esteem, however, you may need to take more serious steps to resolve it.

Once you are able to get beyond unnecessary concern with normal fluctuations, when someone asks you, "How are you doing?" you will be genuinely able to answer, *"Who cares?"* You will know that the more relevant question is, "How are you *playing*?"

On Tilt: Part I

How often do you go on tilt? I have had players tell me they never go on tilt. Usually it has turned out that their definition of tilt and mine differ greatly. They are able to say they don't go on tilt because they define tilt as a major breakdown in play, in which a player goes from reasonable play to the actions of a maniac, or at least a calling station. There's no question that many players are able to avoid this kind of problem entirely, but you are setting your standards too low if you are content simply with staying off this kind of tilt. I use a more precise, yet broader definition of tilt which will be provided shortly. But first, consider an important corollary to the definition which provides a simple way of *identifying* when you have gone on tilt: *Tilt occurs any time you make an incorrect play when you know better.*

If you've been running badly and play a hand that normally you would feel is just barely substandard for the circumstances, and would therefore throw away — that's tilt. If you call someone down with middle pair after he raises you on the turn, rationalizing it with the notion that it sort of looks like he could be bluffing — even though you know he virtually always has a real hand when he raises on the turn — that's tilt. If you make an automatic pilot call on the end after you're raised, just because you've been betting top pair all the way and are frustrated that you could have been drawn out on *again* by a very weak player, that's tilt. The list, of course, could go on, but the idea is that you know better, yet make the play anyway.

Many instances of tilt are quite subtle. If you fail to scrutinize your own play closely, you may not even recognize being on tilt. This is especially so when you have been erring on the incorrect side of some close decisions. (This is virtually always the less conservative side; for, although incorrect, playing too conservatively can rarely be called tilt.). You may, for example, make a call or perhaps a raise which could be correct under

212

similar circumstances, but under *these* circumstances, if you were thinking more objectively, you would realize a fold was, in fact, the better choice. Playing that slightly substandard hand is another example. Though these are near borderline decisions, their cost becomes significant when they are frequent, or when one error compounds itself by leading to another in the same hand. Making an unwarranted bluff on the flop, for example, may lead you to follow through with bluffs on fourth and fifth streets in a futile effort to get an opponent to lay his hand down. When these kinds of misplays are included in a definition of tilt, it becomes clear that there are few players who do not go on tilt at least occasionally. I would guess that fewer than five percent of *professional* players have tilt under such control that they can honestly say that it rarely, if ever, appears in their play.

The cause of any instance of tilt is emotional. This is self evident. Unless you are just goofing around, not trying to play well, what other cause could there be for playing a hand poorly when you know how to play it correctly? Emotion is the trigger. A reaction such as frustration, or feeling demoralized, triggers an impulsive decision to play a hand in a way that you know is incorrect. This leads to my definition of tilt: *Tilt is any adverse impact of emotion on one's play.*

It is widely understood that tilt is nearly always triggered by losing. During a given session it is most likely to occur after losing one or more hands. Looking at your play from a longer term perspective it is highly likely that tilt surfaces most during periods of running badly. When you go for many sessions getting a disproportionate percentage of bad cards, missed draws, and the like, it takes maturity and an exceptional appreciation of the nature of the fluctuations in poker to play on correctly, without reacting emotionally.

It is not easy to estimate the cost of going on tilt. It will vary as a function of frequency of occurrence and of the types of errors you tend to make when emotion affects your play. What is clear though is that most otherwise good players could significantly boost their hourly rates simply by reducing the frequency with which they act on emotion during play. Many players have developed their fluency with poker theory to a far greater extent than their understanding of how and why they go on tilt. Indeed, they are still beginners in their ability to stay off tilt.

I should point out as well that some poor players use tilt as an excuse for their disappointing results. Even if they never went on tilt they would lose, but they would then have to face the truth that tilt allows them to avoid — that they simply don't play well enough to win. For players engaged in such self-deception, some serious self-examination and study of the game will be needed before this essay and the one that follows will be of much help.

If, as is likely, you could stand improvement in this area of your game, then consider applying effort in two areas:

1. **Make sure you have a thorough and accurate understanding of the swings generated by poker play over time.** (I am assuming that you have a solid grasp of the basic odds/probabilities involved in the games you play. If not, then you must establish this basic component of your playing foundation as well.) Read and think about Mason Malmuth's work in this area, as well as everything related to this topic that David Sklansky and Mike Caro have written. If you're ambitious you can also research the topic on Internet poker sites such as the Two Plus Two Forum (go to www.twoplustwo.com and click "Forum") and the newsgroup, rec.gambling.poker. Then go back and look at your own results over a long period of time. (Assuming you keep records.) One easy way to do this is to graph them. This should help clarify your view of the "long run." When you see a graph of a thousand hours of your play you will better understand how pointless it is to fret over how you are doing during a given session. The deeper your understanding of the effects of the chance element in poker, the less likely you are to feel frustrated or victimized by it when it has not worked in your favor for some period of time.

2. **Adopt an active method of preventing yourself from playing on impulse, and for reducing the likelihood that you will go on tilt in the future.** An important step in this direction can involve a conscious shift of focus as you play, as well as an effort to reshape your thinking about your goals during play. Part II of this discussion of tilt will address this step with a description of an attitude which gives many top players significant immunity to tilt while they play.

On Tilt: Part II — The Professional Attitude

In Part One of this two part look at the problem of "tilt" I defined tilt as any adverse impact of emotion on one's play. I encouraged readers to develop a thorough understanding of the monetary swings to be expected in poker as an aide to preventing tilt. This understanding is an integral part of what is presented here — an attitude, possessed by some of the best players, which is completely contrary to acting on emotion during play.

Once we recognize that going on tilt involves the influence of emotion on one's play, we can begin to address the cause of any instance of tilt. Usually one of two things triggers the emotional reaction that creates tilt. Most often it is a downward monetary fluctuation. More rarely it may be an interpersonal experience with another player (e.g., you react angrily to something said by another player, and this affects your play). The idea that runs through this article applies mainly to preventing tilt in response to downward fluctuations. Though it does help somewhat in dealing with interpersonal factors. If you have frequent problems maintaining good play despite what others at the table may say or do, this reflects emotional issues which may require more serious intervention than is offered by any reading material.

Understanding the Professional Attitude

There is an attitude toward the game which can be of great benefit to any poker player. Many excellent players exhibit it to one degree or another, often having developed it naturally, without thinking about it, through experience and study. I believe

216

it can be purposefully developed as well. Once possessed, it strengthens your play immeasurably, particularly your ability to play well regardless of recent results. I call it the "professional" attitude because I see it as the most aware, rational, and sophisticated way by which a winning player can view his results over time. Note however, that simply being a poker professional does not mean you have mastered this attitude. In fact, many professionals do not maintain it very well. I see those few who do as the *most* professional in the business. Note as well, that you certainly need not be a professional player to take advantage of this attitude. I know highly skilled players who do not play for the bulk of their living, but who clearly exhibit the professional attitude.

So what is it? First, the foundation of the professional attitude is an understanding of the principles of correct play paired with an accurate appreciation of the nature of the chance element (particularly the kinds of fluctuations) encountered in poker. Thus, besides knowing how to play well, you must recognize that you will experience random fluctuations of nearly every conceivable variety, restrained only by the standard deviation associated with your play at particular limits, and the upward trend (if you are a winning player) dictated by your hourly rate.

The second element of the professional attitude is the ability to assess your own play and that of your opponents. When you are able to analyze a hand and determine that you have played correctly, that is one step toward being less emotionally invested in whether or not you won the pot. When you are able to identify your opponents' errors and accurately contrast their level of play with your own, you will be able to choose games in which you know you have a positive expectation. Then, when you know you are beating the game in the long run, you will be closer to a healthy indifference toward your short term results.

Professional... NOT!

Before I identify the third and probably most important facet of this attitude, I should mention that it is easy to spot an absence of the professional attitude. When I hear a player complaining about a bad beat, or how bad his luck has been during a session, I know that, at least temporarily, he is out of touch with an accurate appreciation of poker's chance element. Though we all claim to know it, some players seem to need remedial help in truly embracing the fact that bad beats are to be expected, and are just an indication of an opponents' bad play. Have they forgotten that without others' bad play the games would be unbeatable? Similarly, without periods of bad luck, good players would always win, bad players would only lose, and there would be no more games.

Sometimes players who do not possess the professional attitude will try, with the best of intentions, to force their irrational views on you. I recall thinking about this sometime ago during a playing session in which I experienced some unusually large fluctuations. After getting ahead $1,300 in a $15-$30 game, I gradually lost back all but about $100 of the win. Friends who had witnessed the downswing were coming up to me offering words of encouragement. Some suggested I leave before I lost back all of my win. Repeatedly I responded with comments like, "That's just the way it goes sometimes. No big deal. It's a good game; why would I leave?" I had the sense that they felt sorry for me, that they didn't realize that I really *meant* those things. Yes, I was disappointed at my result, but I knew that I had not made any errors that I could identify, and that it was an especially good game. So my disappointment was only mild. I remembered as well a session a couple of months earlier when I had been stuck $1,200, then had a $1,300 upswing to end with a $100 win. As most players would, I had felt good about that result. I realized that on this day I had simply had the same fluctuations in reverse. Had I not kept in mind a clear view of these sorts of facts, supported by an understanding of the nature of poker's fluctuations, I have no doubt that I would have been considerably more upset about the outcome of this session, increasing the chance that emotion would affect my play.

I am not suggesting that it is easy to avoid emotional reactions to downswings. I sometimes struggle with this myself. But to the extent that you can take fluctuations in stride, as natural, unavoidable occurrences, you will bypass the major factor that puts most players on tilt.[30]

You, The Machine

Imagine a computer program of the future, or perhaps some superior "intelligent" creation descended from today's software. Suppose you had such a program running on an equally advanced computer, playing poker for you today in a $20-$40 hold 'em game which went around the clock. Naturally, the program would use highly sophisticated artificial intelligence, observing and listening to the other players with the computer's advanced audio

---

[30] That said, since it is not always possible to completely avoid all emotional involvement in how you are doing in a game, I will pass along a clever idea pointed out to me by David Sklansky in discussing this essay. The idea is that there is really nothing wrong with, and may be benefits associated with making a *slightly* incorrect play if it might substantially cut your loss. For instance, you might play a small pair with one opponent fewer than you normally require, or draw to a gutshot straight with slightly insufficient pot odds. Neither of these is going to cost more than a tiny bit in the long run, but either may win you a decent pot and lift your spirits, thus helping you continue to play your best. This is especially applicable to hold 'em where you always have the dubious chance to see whether you would have made your hand, and will thus likely be further demoralized if you see that, for the sake of perfect play, you missed your chance to get close to even.

and video capabilities, always determining the best play based on all available information. While you sat home, the computer, starting with a generous $30,000 bankroll, would play, always with an extremely advanced level of "skill." Because it would play better than any human it could be expected to achieve an hourly rate of somewhere over two big bets per hour, the exact rate determined by how tough the game was over time.

Most knowledgeable players would see such a situation as a virtual guarantee of making good money over time. There would of course be some periodic downswings, but they would always be overcome. This would be a "sure thing" if there ever was one.

Now imagine that although you would spend most of your time in other pursuits, you could, at any time, turn on a monitor and check in on how your computer was faring in the game. Let's say the computer has been playing for several months, and has generated something near the expected profit for that time span. Now, at 1:35 pm on a Monday you check in and learn that the computer was just drawn out on by a player who had only two outs. In fact it has sustained a $960 downswing over the last few hours, having been similarly drawn out on several times and after missing a number of big draws of its own. Do you worry? Are you upset? Most good players would answer something like, "Of course not. That machine will just keep playing and eventually win more than any other player in the game."[31]

Yet many of these same good players, become sullen and feel dejected when they sit through a similar downswing during their own play. For many it affects their play, only making matters worse. You must realize that as long as you continue to play as correctly as you can, given the information available to you, you are really quite similar to the computer. You aren't quite as skilled, so your hourly rate will be lower, but as long as you have an adequate bankroll and play in games in which you have a positive expectation, you will win over time, just like the

---

[31] This frame of mind is not as hypothetical as it seems. Most casino owners possess it as we speak.

computer. So the next time you are stuck or have lost back a good win, think of yourself as a computer, playing on, playing correctly, hand after hand in a game that never ends.[32] Rest assured, if you are good enough to win, you will win over time. Poker is tough enough; don't make it harder on yourself by going on tilt in response to natural variations in the cards.

Danger in the Goal of Winning?

Aside from it's skill, the great strength of the computer program I described above is that it has only one purpose: To play very well. That's all it does. It is incapable of tilt. It doesn't try to get even, it doesn't get mad and try to beat a specific player, it doesn't worry about losing back a win. It just plays on, expertly. In so doing it beats us all. It possesses the professional attitude to an inhuman degree.

Though you are human, by adopting the professional attitude to the extent that you can, you can separate yourself from the poker crowd. Only a tiny fraction of players truly embrace it. Perhaps the single greatest obstacle to it arises from what is for most players the very essence of poker: Winning and losing. Most players naturally see poker as a competition, a game they try to win. Just one tiny step further, and winning becomes their primary focus as they play. That's the problem. By fixing their focus on winning (in the short run) they concern themselves with what they hope will happen in the future. Yet they are constantly confronted with decisions in the present. Moreover, it is their handling of those decisions which determines their long term results. Their focus is thus misplaced.

Please don't misunderstand me. Certainly any serious player aims to win in the long run. There's no need to deny your reason

---

[32] Bear in mind that if your are losing, and this causes your opponents to respond to you differently, you may need to adjust your play.

for sitting down at the poker table to begin with, but beware of confusing your long and short tem goals. Focusing your attention strongly on winning in the short term will promote tilt and damage your results.

What, you don't believe me? Then try this sometime. For an hour of your play stop thinking about the decisions you face at the poker table. Don't assess your options as you play each hand. Put those things out of your mind. Shift your focus instead to your desire to win as soon as possible this session. You want to win *each pot right now.* Put your mind intensely and exclusively on winning them. Now, how well do you think you'll play during this hour? I can tell you I don't like your chances.

Well, though few players take their minds *that* far off their playing decisions, I hope that scenario makes clear that it is really only on the objective assessment of those decisions that your mind belongs as you play.

The Golden Key

We have come to what I see as the central feature of the professional attitude: *The awareness of the need to focus not on short term results, but on the quality of your play.* This is really a golden key to consistently good poker. Made possible by the elements described above, adherence to this focus will help maximize your hourly rate and provide you with substantial immunity to tilt. When your attention is focused in this manner, you do not think, "Unbelievable, she drew out on me again! Now I'm stuck so bad it'll be a miracle if I get even." You think, "She was semi-bluffing with her flush draw. I think I charged her as much as I could by raising on the turn. Was there a better way to play it?… Next hand." You don't think, "I'm tired of being stuck. I'm going to play this little suited connector even though it may not be correct in this spot. Maybe I'll win a big pot." You think, "Not profitable here. I fold."

Thus, while your long term goal of winning remains, your focus in the present becomes simply playing well. Of course playing well means making as much money as possible over time. So it is intimately linked with winning *in the long run*. It makes great sense, in fact, to think of your decisions in terms of monetary expectation or "expected value" (EV), to use current Internet parlance. You strive to make the decision which will average the most profit in the long run, but, that is not thinking about winning per se. It is not thinking about competition, or victory, or defeat. It is analyzing decisions.

I would even suggest that you will do best if you can simply put winning out of your mind as you play. Your long term goal exists, but forget about it for the time being. Put it aside and think only about your play. Make playing well, playing to maximize EV, your only purpose at the table.[33]

There are a great many skilled players whose results at poker are nevertheless poor simply because they are out of touch with the professional attitude. They get caught up in concerns over having winning sessions, go on tilt, and their judgment becomes impaired over prolonged periods. Ironically, there are less skilled players who do better at the game simply because they maintain the professional attitude very consistently.

If you have any problem with emotion affecting your play, try shifting your focus away from short term results to the quality of your play. Work on your fluency with poker theory. Keep in mind that short term fluctuations of all sorts are inevitable. Analyze your play and that of your opponents. Once the professional attitude is your natural state at the table, you will be tilt resistant. Moreover, your mental energy will be objectively focused where it will do you the most good — on the decisions which determine your long term earnings.

---

[33] Note that some otherwise good players go on tilt when they are playing at a limit that is too high for their bankroll. Under these circumstances the threat of a loss preoccupies them and makes it especially difficult to focus only on the quality of their play. The solution, of course, is to play at a lower limit.

Subtle Losses
of Judgement: Part I

This is a topic to which few poker writers have devoted much attention, but which is of critical importance to players who want to do well at poker. Some years ago, not long after moving up from $6-$12 to $10-$20 hold 'em, I mentioned to a friend who was (and still is) one of the steadiest professional players I have known, that I'd had a bad month. He responded, "Well, there are times when *God* couldn't win, but more often than not, when you look at a bad month, it turns out you had something to do with it." For most players I am sure that his observation is correct. This essay is about what I believe is frequently going on when an otherwise good player has "something to do with it."

Consider the decisions made over the course of a few poker sessions. For a knowledgeable, experienced player, most are fairly straight forward if not automatic. You fold a lot of hands without a second thought, you make some obvious folds on the flop or turn, you bet some hands straight through with out having to deal with anything very complex or unclear. Of course not all of poker is that easy. As you know, within those few sessions you will inevitably be confronted with difficult decisions as well, but those obviously difficult decisions are not the only ones that present problems; for among the normally simple, straight forward decisions lies a class of decisions with a special character. If you are a very good player these are relatively easy, clear decisions as long as your judgment is unimpaired. However, they are instances in which, if anything interferes with your judgment, it is easy to rationalize the wrong decision.

Thus, any interference with the application of sound judgment affects not only difficult decisions, but these routine, easily rationalized decisions as well. Probably the best known interference is frank "tilt" or "steaming," but I suspect even more damaging to the long term results of most better players are more subtle phenomena (including subtle varieties of tilt) which diminish good judgment at the poker table. I submit that a large percentage of players who have learned enough to play quite well damage their results by occasionally, subtly, and often unknowingly, making their playing decisions in the absence of their normal best judgment. They sometimes play with this subtly impaired judgment over many playing sessions, rationalizing incorrect decisions and severely cutting into their profits.

Making Profitable Decisions

Let's look at two key requirements for making profitable decisions in poker:
1. You must have a good knowledge of poker.
2. You must exercise consistently good judgment in your poker decisions.

Obviously, if you don't have a reasonable understanding of poker strategy, at least on an "intuitive" level, you will not be able to play well. You also need good judgment. An understanding of theory enables you to identify the elements you need to consider to make sound poker decisions. But upon considering those elements you must frequently exercise *judgment* to make the best possible decision.

Here's a simple example. Say you hold a strong hand and are considering whether to bet or to check-raise an opponent on the river in hold 'em. First, your knowledge of poker theory allows you to identify these two options as your best choices. Then, in assessing the merits of each, it further tells you that you need to consider the likelihood your opponent will call if you bet, the chance he will bet if you check, and the subsequent chance he will call if you raise. To assess these final three variables you must rely not so much on your knowledge of theory, but on your own best guesses, and your judgment about this player concerning each of those questions.

Good judgement in poker derives in part from innate talent, personality type, and emotional maturity. To a large extent you can also develop it through the interplay of experience and continual analysis of your play. In time your efforts pay off in more reliable judgment for most situations. A variety of factors can, however, interfere with judgment in subtle ways, nudging you just outside of the zone of correct play.

Enemies of Sound Judgment

A number of factors, apart from obvious tilt, may interfere with a player's judgment enough to do serious damage to his poker results. At some risk of oversimplifying the phenomenon, I suggest that the following ideas capture much of what usually happens. Certainly elements other than those I will list can impair judgement in poker. Here are three which I believe are especially important. These ideas derive from analysis of my own experience as well as discussion with and observation of skilled players exhibiting this problem.

1. **Habitual play.** One insidious threat to sound judgment in poker is the adoption of habitual ways of playing hands. Sometimes these are correct under the conditions in which they develop. Game conditions may change, however, making the same plays now incorrect.

    If, for instance, you are playing regularly against several very aggressive players and habitual bluffers — note that sometimes the distinction between the two is blurry — as well as a couple of "weak tight" players, you will learn to call down the aggressive players with modest holdings fairly frequently. Simultaneously you will know to fold the same hands when bet into by the weak tight players. In neither case are you required to exercise a great deal of judgement. In fact, you may find that you have almost put this aspect of your play on "auto-pilot," automatically calling here, folding there, because you have analyzed your opponents' styles and little additional thinking is needed. The trap is that if you move on to a different game containing different types of players, or there is some turn over in the regular players in your game, you may forget to turn off the auto-pilot. It is all too easy to continue making the plays you have become accustomed to, without applying considered judgment to the changed conditions in which you now find yourself. In this case you might quickly and incorrectly label your new opponents as "bluffers" or "non-bluffers," because that is what you are used to, failing to consider that they might in fact lie somewhere in between. Eventually, when you realize that you seem to keep "zigging when you should zag," you may take a step back and analyze what you have been doing wrong. In the meantime you will cost yourself some money.[34]

Habitual play can also arise from excessive adherence to a "cookbook" approach to the game. You have determined some effective plays for negotiating a variety of situations, but poker is a game of continual adjustment and counter-adjustment between observing opponents. Any plays that you make without variation, are vulnerable to exploitation by those who notice. Thus, the real problem develops when your good, profitable plays become so habitual, so automatic for you, that they make you more readable. It is certainly easier to play in a rote, automatic way, but the routine failure to apply judgement to individual situations will cost you.

2. **Subtle tilt.** Another kind of lapse in judgment is seen in the subtler varieties of tilt. (We have already discussed less subtle varieties.) These can be triggered by a losing streak. If an otherwise solid player becomes repeatedly frustrated (or in some other way distressed) about his poor results, the

---

[34] It can also happen that those *same* players have moved into different categories as they have changed stakes.

frustration can become an ongoing problem, threatening to interfere with judgment and affect his play on a continuing basis. If you find that over multiple sessions you are preoccupied with the "bad beats" you have taken or the bad cards you have been receiving, this problem may be close at hand. Some typical responses, for a better player, are to begin playing a few sub-marginal hands that he normally would fold, to overplay some hands (e.g., raising when he should call or fold), and to go too far in calling with hands, perhaps rationalizing his calls with unfounded suspicions that his opponents are bluffing, or pushing weak hands.

More generally, anything which shifts your focus strongly away from the quality of your play to your short term results is likely to trigger subtle tilt. This can range from concerns over "quitting winners" to feeling competitive with certain players. These are foci which only distract from the precise judgment needed to make consistently correct decisions. Subtle tilt is a broad category, encompassing any adverse, subtle impact of emotion on your play.

3. **Misinformation.** A third enemy of sound judgment is any misconception that a player may adopt about what constitutes profitable play. These can start with something you might read or hear from another player. If it is incorrect, or you misinterpret it, then acting on it is likely to cost you. For instance, you might hear from a skilled player that "Good players can play some lesser hands because they outplay opponents after the flop." While there is some truth in this, it is dangerously easy to take the idea too far (particularly in hold 'em), using it to rationalize the play of hands that dip below "marginal." Similarly, I frequently see poker advice on the Internet which is submitted very confidently and articulately, and eagerly accepted as correct by players hungry for knowledge. Unfortunately, despite its attractive packaging, the advice is often inaccurate. You must assess very carefully any poker advice that comes from a source you

are not sure of, including making sure you understand correctly what that person said.

Often, plays made in the absence of optimum judgment may be just barely wrong. For this reason they can be difficult to spot in your play, and may persist for some time. Because they are made repeatedly, and because some are errors which compound themselves during a hand, the cost can add up significantly. A vicious cycle may develop with your poor results increasing your frustration, and leading to even worse play.

It can also happen that these enemies of sound judgment work in combination. For example, being subtly on tilt for a period of multiple sessions, your errors may become habitual, especially if they are reinforced by some short term winning results. You may then have great trouble seeing them as incorrect even after you have resolved the emotional factors underlying the tilt. This is an insidious process indeed.

In Part II, I will describe some typical errors which result from these subtle losses of judgement in poker.

Subtle Losses
of Judgement: Part II

In Part I we examined some factors that cause subtle damage to judgment in poker. I listed habitual play, subtle tilt, and misinformation as "enemies of sound judgment." In addition, I touched briefly on some of the errors players make as a consequence of these factors. Now let's look at these errors a bit more closely.

Typical Resulting Errors

1. **Playing extra hands.** This is one of the easiest errors to fall prey to when your judgment is slightly impaired. There are a number of reasons for this. It is all too easy to rationalize playing substandard hands in hold 'em. You can tell yourself, "The very best players play some extra hands and, hey, I really am a good player. I probably *should* be playing these hands." You can give too little credit to your opponents, thereby convincing yourself that they are so unskilled that you can play more hands against them. It is, of course, also easy to simply to give in to temptation with a slightly sub-marginal hand in the hope of turning around a downswing.[35]

    Adding to any of the above contributors to poor hand selection can be misinformation, or a simple lack of knowledge. Even fairly good players often lack sufficient knowledge of hand selection to make correct decisions consistently in less routine situations. The result can be that errors which seem trivial preflop are compounded as you get

---

[35] The psychologist in me can't help pointing out that this is really the hope of easing some distressing emotion.

into trouble on the later streets, or are made so frequently that their cost cuts significantly into your hourly rate.

2.   **Calling opponents down too much.** This is one of the most common effects of diminished judgment in poker play. It is a good example of the kind of play that can become habitual. We all enjoy picking off a bluff, but it is possible to get into a mode of too frequently thinking your opponents are trying to steal the pot from you. So you become something of a calling station whenever you have a hand like middle or bottom pair. How does this develop? In hold 'em the seed for its development is learning that often none of the players in a pot flops much. Having a period of repeated success at catching bluffers can then set the tendency in motion. It may also result from subtle tilt. Frustrated, you put the desire to win pots ahead of the goal of playing well, and, so you begin to "call 'em down," trying to win any pot you possibly can.

   Of course becoming a habitual caller will prove terribly costly. When you are playing with your best judgment you carefully pick your spots to call a player down with a weak hand. When your judgment has lapsed, you may do it more indiscriminately. For example, say you are in the big blind with:

Two players call, as does the small blind. The flop is:

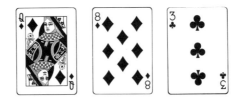

The small blind bets. He is a player who bluffs excessively when he's stuck, but is currently not stuck, and is playing his "A" game. You raise. The other players fold. Now the small blind reraises. Given no further information, if you are a good player, playing with sound judgment, you will probably either fold now or take a card off and fold if faced with another bet if you haven't improved. However, if your judgment has eroded, and you have developed the "call 'em down" syndrome, you may well go to the river. Perhaps with the rationalization, "Well, this guy really bluffs a lot sometimes. He may really just be on a draw." Then you will probably be shown a hand like

or two pair.

When your judgment is sharp it is easy to see the folly of such habitual calling. But when you have left your better judgment behind such play never seems far wrong — at least while you are engaged in it. You know you are taking a risk, but you can justify (i.e., rationalize) it; and you know one thing is *certain*: You *might* win the pot.

3. **Ignoring negation of outs.** "Negation of outs" is simply a phrase I use to refer to circumstances suggesting that some or all of your outs may not be good if they hit. For instance, when you have overcards like

the flop is

and there's a bet and a raise ahead of you, it is easy to see that your "outs" are negated, to one degree or another, by the various hands opponents may hold (or draws they may complete) which beat any one pair. Of course it's usually not that obvious. Consistently recognizing when your outs are significantly negated, and playing accordingly, is one of the marks of a skilled player. Likewise, failing to recognize the negation of outs is a mark of poor play.

Sometimes however, even good players slip into a tendency to ignore, or fail to accurately assess the negation of outs. This can easily come about as a result of subtle tilt. A player may know, under normal conditions, that some or all of his outs are likely to be no good even if they hit. If his play is emotionally affected he may rationalize playing on, talking himself into a read on his opponent's hand which suggests that his outs are good.

For example, say you are dealt

and open for a raise with three people left to act behind you. Only the small blind, an average player, calls. Now the flop comes:

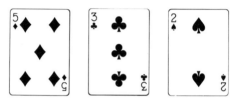

Your opponent checks and calls your bet. The turn brings the

Your opponent checks again and you opt to bet. When you do, he raises. Normally, thinking completely objectively, you would know that you couldn't assume you had seven outs (four for the gutshot draw and three aces). While your opponent may be semi-bluffing, or has a hand which does indeed give you seven outs, you would know, depending on the opponent, that there is some chance he could have hands ranging from AQ, or AA (the latter having been slowplayed preflop) to A4s, 55, 33, or 22. These hands reduce your outs to either four or three (the latter giving you only half the pot).

(You can figure precisely the number of hands your opponent might have that preserve your outs versus those that negate them by counting combinations. Sklansky outlines this procedure in *Poker, Gaming, & Life*. In this example, however, it is clear without even bothering with this, that your outs are significantly negated.) Thus, while seven outs is about a 6-to-1 shot, the 6.5-to-1 you are getting from this pot is not enough to call. You cannot win this pot the one time out of seven that the "6-to-1" figure refers to.

If your judgment is clouded by emotion or otherwise hindered, then it will be easy to convince yourself that you do have all seven of those outs. You may decide that your opponent is semi-bluffing, despite this being an "average" player whose likelihood of making this check-raise without a made hand is minuscule. You may put him on a hand like

somehow "sensing" that that is "definitely" what he has, thereby ignoring the other possibilities which are, in fact, quite real.

It is crucial to good play that you stay constantly aware of negation of outs. I believe that ignoring this concept is one of the most common manifestations of the subtle losses of judgment that poker players experience. Of course, you must not bend over backward in the other direction and constantly convince yourself that your opponents have hands that have you drawing dead. That would just be playing scared or "weak-tight." What's needed is an objective awareness of when some or all of your outs may be negated. If you find over some period of time that many of your errors involve calls where you may have ignored the negation of outs, you may be able to bring your play back into a more profitable zone simply through a renewed awareness of this concept.

4.   **Overplaying hands.** This can evolve out of a player's efforts to play better and extract more profit from hands played. He rightly takes to heart the importance of aggressive play. The problem occurs when he fails to see where to draw the line. He may misconstrue the advice he has seen, or may be heeding advice that was too narrowly focused on the importance of aggression. In these cases, he is acting on the basis of a kind of misinformation.

Alternatively, subtle tilt may of course be the culprit. In any case, it is not hard to rationalize crossing the line of correct play by too often raising when a call or a fold is preferable.

As an example of overplaying a hand, say you are dealt

before the flop. You raise in an early position, a weak player in a middle position calls, as does a player in late position. You are unfamiliar with the late position player. The blinds fold. The flop comes:

You bet, the first player calls, and the second player raises. You reraise, the weak player calls, and the unfamiliar player caps it at four bets. How do you play from here? Remember that you don't know this player.

Options you might consider include:

A. Folding right there. (I hope you wouldn't seriously consider this option given your pot odds at this point.)
B. Calling with the intention of checking and folding if you don't improve and he bets on the turn.
C. Calling with the intention of betting out on the turn provided the turn card does not appear to have completed a draw for the raiser.
D. Calling with the intention of calling him down if you fail to improve, and no scare cards or subsequent action force you to fold.
E. Calling with the intention of check-raising on the turn whether or not you improve.

Without getting into the correct play, option "E" would be overplaying the hand against a "typical," unfamiliar player. It would not be a terrible error, for you might in fact have the best hand and extract maximum profit by playing it this way. It would not be a big surprise to see a skilled player choose this option, but it would indicate that he had strayed slightly out of the zone of correct play as a result of some diminution of judgment. It would often indicate a bit of tilt. Under different circumstances, his awareness of the strong chance he is beaten at this point, and will have to improve to win, would guide him away from this option.

5. **Making too many fancy plays.** This is another error that may arise out of misinformed efforts to play well. A player reaches a certain level of competence and asks, "Where do I go from here?" Making more and more fancy plays may seem like a logical choice. Such fancy play can easily become habitual — habitual slowplaying, habitual use of unusual plays… . This turns costly as it takes the place of careful judgment in individual situations. Deception and

unconventional plays have their place, but used indiscriminately they dilute your results.

Conclusion

If you have good reason to believe that you are capable of a certain hourly rate, but your results over a subsequent (sufficiently long) period are disappointing, one explanation to rule out is that you have been playing with subtly impaired judgment. As a conscientious player you should frequently monitor your play for the errors I have described, as well as others which reflect diminished judgment.[36] Your ability to recognize errors will be limited by your knowledge of poker theory. By analyzing your play and looking for evidence of subtle losses of judgment, you will improve your chance of playing consistently at your best.

---

[36] I have certainly not exhausted the list of errors which players make when their judgment is subtly impaired. Different players stray from sound play in different ways. Any category of poker error may be involved. Another common and important category, for instance, is calling when you should raise. Consistently playing too passively in this way means making pot costing errors — a very costly problem.

A Poker Player in Therapy

In the preceding essays I defined "tilt" as *any adverse impact of emotion on one's play*. The ideas offered should help many players who apply them seriously to avoid or counteract the emotional reactions that we call "going on tilt." This can mean a substantial improvement in their long term profits from poker. For some though, my advice, or that of anyone else, will be insufficient to remedy their problems with tilt. As one trained in clinical psychology, I will say that in some cases the only remedy I am aware of would come from addressing the tilt problem in psychotherapy. The reason other avenues fail (if the tilt problem is severe or persistent enough) is that the emotional reactions we call "tilt" often involve elements hidden from consciousness. Without putting some time into one or another of a few different kinds of therapy, it is almost impossible to develop real insight into or to achieve any resolution of these unconscious factors. Though such a solution to a tilt problem may sound extreme, it is actually quite cost effective when you consider the likely savings (from reducing tilt), especially for a serious middle or higher limit player.

Even the less serious, "garden variety" tilt of typical players involves emotional factors which tend to remain hidden in everyday life outside the walls of the therapist's office. Thus, briefly putting on my psychologist's hat, I would like to suggest that we are all creatures of emotion. Emotions influence a great deal of our behavior. Difficulties arise, when we are unaware of the true cause of an emotional reaction. For example, you can become anxious about something without really knowing why. Similarly, psychotherapists frequently see patients who are depressed, but don't know why. (Of course there is the "experience versus chemistry" debate, but I'll keep this simple.) Their task is, in large part, to help these patients come to a deep understanding and appreciation of the experiences that ultimately led to a depressive reaction.

In poker, when a player experiences a sizable downswing or perhaps a very "bad beat," which might even be compounded by his opponent needling him afterward, it is not surprising that this player might react with feelings of anger, a desire to seek revenge, even various palpable bodily feelings and a noticeable interference by emotions with cognition.

If you experience this, the real question is, "Why are you really angry?" To answer this question you almost have to have spent a couple of years or so in one of a few kinds of psychotherapy. You have to have repeatedly experienced the process of looking beneath the surface emotion to determine what *other* (deeper, if you will) emotions and cognition's are fueling the feelings of which you are aware (e.g., the anger and desire for revenge). Once you have gained an understanding of what's going on under the surface, the troublesome emotion tends to dissipate. You regain your objectivity.

Though it is probably not necessary for large numbers of players to enter therapy to deal with their tilt problems, I thought it might be of some value to try to illustrate something of the sorts of unconscious emotional elements that may underlie tilt by giving just a glimpse at how they might emerge in therapy. Such factors are present even for very "normal" players. It is just that they lack the intensity, or perhaps the precise quality which plagues the more seriously tilt-prone player.

To try to illustrate this I will use a very brief fictitious interchange that could conceivably take place between a therapist and patient in a session in which the patient has complained of going on tilt in a recent poker session. He had taken a "bad beat" and had been laughed at by his opponent afterward. (Note that the patient in this example would be one who has been in therapy for some time, and so is relatively efficient at getting in touch with feelings and verbalizing them. Nevertheless, it is much more condensed than is typical in real life. It is intended as well to represent a relatively "normal" person. In writing it I had in mind the kinds of internal difficulties with which many typical players might wrestle.)

Patient: Yeah, it was bad enough to lose that much in the hand, but when he sat there and giggled I *really* got angry.

Therapist: I can hear in your voice that you're still furious.

Patient: That jerk; I could have k-...

Therapist: You could have killed him.

Patient: Yeah. I really wanted to. So I tried to really get him back a few hands later, but it just backfired. He had a real hand and I overplayed mine. God, I was just so mad.

Therapist: I think you felt more than just mad. How did you feel when he started giggling?

Patient: Well, angry, but uhm...

Therapist: What else?

Patient: Hmm, I guess I really felt sort of demeaned.

Therapist: What did you hear him saying to you with his giggling?

Patient: Well, I guess it was like he was saying, "You're nothing. Fool, I just stomped on you in that hand."

Therapist: Like he was belittling you.

Patient: Yeah. Like he was just spitting on me or on any ability I have as a poker player.

Therapist: Your ability as a poker player is something you're proud of. You really have some of your self-esteem invested in it. And it was like he was just laughing at it. Made you feel like a nothing.

Patient: Yes, and I felt like everyone else there had to be seeing me as a real chump.

Therapist: How so?

Patient: Well, like they saw him really stick it to me and so they probably saw me as just this poor defeated victim or something.

Therapist: Do you think that's how they really saw you? Tell me, if you saw one player draw out with such a longshot as that on another player, what would you be thinking?

Patient: Heh. Guess I'd be thinking about how badly the winner had played, what a clueless player he is. Okay, I see your point.

Therapist: Tell me, when he giggled, and you felt as demeaned as you described, did that feel anything like the occasions you've described in the past, when your dad used to tease you in front of the rest of your family?

And so on. The idea is simply that there is often more involved than is readily apparent on the surface. To the extent that we can observe in ourselves what is really fueling our intense surface reactions, we will have more of a handle on them, and they less of a handle on us. Though it is not expected to transform anyone, I hope this brief illustration helps foster some appreciation for the depth of what may really be occurring when you "go off" following a bad beat or a frustrating downswing.

Poker and Emotion

Afterthought

Clearly, you cannot afford to act on upsetting emotions during play. This does not mean denying all feelings. Ideally, a very emotionally well adjusted player with a healthy self-esteem *and* a deep understanding of the nature of the chance element and fluctuations involved in poker, will simply not react with the kinds of emotions that cause tilt. He will instead respond productively with healthy emotions to his awareness of the quality of his play. However, the unavoidable swings in poker can wear on anyone, and most players need to expend a little effort to avoid sometimes acting on the wrong feelings. Perhaps these suggestions will help you in that effort.

Bear in mind that it is not enough simply to have read and understood the essays. It also takes a consistent, conscious intent to implement the ideas presented. In time, though, they will become automatic enough that you need not keep them constantly at the forefront of your thoughts. Still, do not abandon them if you do not look forward to a return visit from the tilt monster. Whether from frank tilt or a more prolonged, subtle loss of judgment, the adverse impact of emotion on poker decisions is best conscientiously avoided.

Part Five

Miscellaneous Topics

Miscellaneous Topics
Introduction

Here now are three essays which won't help your poker game, but which will make interesting reading nonetheless. With the increased popularity of tournaments, a notable percentage of poker players now prefer and specialize in these events rather than in live games. Players like to debate the merits of one versus the other. Since I have some thoughts on this too, I decided to share them with you here. If you are a devoted tournament player please do not take my comments as a personal affront. I respect the skill of the accomplished tournament player, and am not critical of tournaments in and of themselves, but, as you will see, I do have some concerns.

The other two essays here touch on risk-reward ratios outside poker, and the effects of poker books and articles on the games. Though few would argue that the former deals with the more important topic, I'm sure the latter will draw the most dissenting response. Perhaps I could have fused the two topics; for as you will see, I view the risks and rewards of poker writing in a different way from many serious players.

Why I Don't
Play Tournaments

Poker tournaments are quite popular these days. Entries in the larger tournaments run well into the hundreds. There are players who specialize in and make a living playing these events (though fewer than it would appear). You can win tens and occasionally hundreds of thousands of dollars if you win a tournament event. But for as long as I've played poker I've hardly ever played in them, preferring instead to stick to live games. Here's why:

Punching the Time Clock

Partly, it's for the same reason that I currently choose to devote most of my time to poker rather than to a traditional job. When I first became interested in poker I was drawn to the freedom to set my own hours, to come and go as I pleased. I liked the idea of making my "office" here one day, somewhere else the next, depending on game selection factors, or just my mood. I still like these things. With poker, I have a sense of freedom, an ability to create my own lifestyle, which I think is not as easy to achieve in many other fields.

Much of that would be taken away if I were to focus seriously on tournaments. To play a tournament you have to be at the casino at a certain time. You have to stay until you bust out or win. If you're serious about it you have to travel to go to the bigger tournaments. These things are not at all attractive to someone who, when he first saw the title to John Fox's book, *Play Poker, Quit Work, and Sleep Till Noon*, said, "Hey, that's for me!"

To be independent from the constraints of mainstream work structures, yet to feel the gratification of work performed expertly — these are the things sought by many a serious live game player.

To play the tournament circuit is to take one step back toward the structured, scheduled ways of the conventional working world.

Are Tournaments Poker?

On a technical level, there are serious differences between tournament and live game play. While it is an exaggeration to say that tournaments are not poker, I do see the point made by those who hold that view. Tournaments put much weight on a small set of skills which have little to do with success in live games. Often, for instance, they reward a level of aggression which would lead to disaster in live games. In tournaments such play takes advantage of opponents who are playing extremely tightly at the wrong times. They further require adjustments of strategy as a function of stack size, the stage of the tournament, and the number of players left. Expertise in these areas is evidently so important in tournaments that at times it appears to almost supersede knowledge of the game itself.[37] I believe this, along with the greater short term luck factor of tournaments (see below), helps explain the not so rare phenomenon of the experienced tournament player who, has rarely if ever played a certain form of poker, entering and winning a tournament event in that game.

To me, the skill of basing strategy on one's own stack size in relation to that of others, while somewhat interesting, is a distraction from more interesting aspects of poker. However, the

---

[37] Note that I say *"evidently"* so important. I am not an expert on tournament strategy, and so am not positive of this statement. Evidence, (including the live game playing styles of a number of well known tournament pros) does point in that direction. Some might argue that the big name tournament players who play with a hyper-aggressive style do not actually win very much in the long run. Their style simply produces enough first place wins to make their names well known. I do not think anyone has shown this assertion to be either true or false.

premium put on aggressive play, avoiding confrontations, and other distinct tournament strategies seems a quirky phenomenon in which I have little interest. My interest lies in poker well played, not in the exploitation of these odd little tournament-specific factors.

The difference in skills required for tournaments and live games also provides one reason why few top tournament players are known also to be excellent players in live games. (Another reason is simply the better hourly rate attainable in higher limit live games.) Many of the most prominent tournament champions are, in fact, well known as "live ones" in ring games. They try to do in the live games what works for them in tournaments, only to have it backfire on them in live play.

Of course there are a select few players who have done well in both tournaments and live games. This is because they have made the effort to develop the skills each requires. They are not good at one merely because they are good at the other. That said, I would argue that it should be easier for a good live game player to become a good tournament player than the other way around. I believe a tournament player whose overall poker skills are merely decent, but whose understanding of and abilities in specific tournament tactics is excellent, can do reasonably well in tournaments. Clearly though, such a player would struggle in live games. Success at live games requires the full development of a broad array of poker skills. These can be quite difficult to master. On the other hand, the skills unique to tournaments are not terribly complex or difficult to acquire. Thus, it should be a simpler task for a skilled live game player to become proficient in the limited set of additional skills required for tournament play, than for a tournament specialist to gain expertise in the large set of skills needed for success in live games.

Tournaments differ from live games also in their short term chance element. It is well known that there is usually a lot of luck involved in winning a given tournament. Sometimes a player has a lucky streak of tournaments, and wins several in a short period of time. Alternatively, even an exceptionally good tournament player can play a great many events without ever placing in the money. (For more see the essay, "Is Your Wallet Fat Enough for Tournaments?" in Sklansky's *Poker, Gaming, & Life.*) Playing the "circuit" as a professional tournament player, going for months at a time with no income at all, perhaps seeking backers, living in hotels, hoping for that next big score to tide me over is, to me, hardly an appealing notion. In live game play something resembling steady income is quite likely for a very good player. Nothing of the sort can be had on the tournament circuit, even for the very best players.

Are They Bad for Poker?

Finally, I have to agree with those who have suggested that, on the whole, tournaments may be bad for poker. When someone wins a large tournament a sizable chunk of money is suddenly removed from the poker economy. Yes, sometimes it may find it's way back if the tournament winner uses it to play live games or more tournaments, but that will not always happen. Frequently — especially with players who are not professional tournament players — that money will be spent on expensive items, never to be converted into chips again. When a player wins the same amount in live games it will generally be in smaller pieces over a period of time. Those small pieces are much more likely to be put back into play. A $30,000 tournament win might buy a new car, but a $1,000 dollar win in a ring game will more likely buy some more buy-ins.[38]

Although any tournament may bring a few people into a cardroom who might not go there otherwise, I think this benefit is outweighed by the problem I have cited. I therefore suspect that poker might be better off without so many tournaments. I do however, think that both very small buy-in tournaments and

---

[38] This argument is similar to the one Mike Caro has used in analyzing the cost of jackpots to the poker economy.

events big enough to attract the media may help bring new players to the game. Thus, it is the scores of medium sized buy-in tournaments that I would contend hurt poker.

I have also observed that many tournament specialists play very little in live games. I have to wonder how many more live games there would be if tournaments were not there to distract players away from them.

I understand that many players very much enjoy tournaments, and I do not mean to disparage their efforts or skills, but as a live game player I am concerned about the degree to which they remove players and money from regular poker games. That is my bias. Could a tournament player turn the tables and criticize live games for taking money and players away from tournaments? Perhaps. But were it not for live games, the foundation of public poker, would tournaments even exist?

Risk (of Death)
— Reward Ratios

Studious gamblers learn to assess carefully the risk-reward ratios in their chosen gambling activities. When the degree of risk is justified by the value of the reward, the skilled gambler takes that risk. Consider the skilled poker player. When he can only beat a bluff, and on the river the pot is offering him 9-to-1, he makes the call if he believes the odds against his opponent bluffing are no greater than 9-to-1. Below 9-to-1, the risk-reward ratio is favorable. If he has assessed the situation correctly, the player is risking the amount of his call, for a reward which will average more than that. (In practice, many good players assess risk-reward more by *feel* than through such an explicit analysis. Nevertheless, they develop considerable skill at doing so. They develop a keen sense of risk-reward ratios without always thinking them through arithmetically.)

A good poker player who has learned to think effectively from a risk-reward point of view has acquired a valuable skill to apply to other areas of life as well. This should be especially true in cases where the player has learned to *think through* risk-reward assessments. That is, skilled players, particularly those who have thought about and studied the game enough that their decisions are frequently fairly conscious, not dictated by unarticulated feel alone, should be able to apply their ability to assess risk and reward with some success to other decisions in their lives. Whether or not a particular player actually does this is another question. Personality traits or other factors may prevent him from doing so. Nevertheless, he does posses skills that are transferable to areas outside poker.

Lets look at three decisions where a sound assessment of risk-reward ratios could help out:

1. **Selecting a Car.** When someone chooses a car to buy, they usually base their decision on such factors as price, performance, safety, looks, and reliability. Performance, looks, and reliability represent much of the "reward" a car can offer. Price, and especially safety, represent the degree of "risk." We have all seen the statistics that show the very real risk we are taking each time we sit behind the wheel of a car. Because automobile safety is related to a very great risk, the risk of losing one's life, it makes sense to consider the risk-reward ratio presented by any car you might purchase.

    Though the degree to which you value your life is a personal matter, I suspect most people do not put sufficient thought into this assessment. Given the great value most people put on their own lives, if they did think about it they would choose safer cars. This is because unless you do not actually put great value on your life, or you put tremendous value on good looking, high performance cars, the rewards offered by any great looking performance car are hardly enough to justify even a small increase in your chance of death (or serious injury). Accordingly, it makes great sense simply to choose the safest car you can afford. Yes, paying more means greater risk of a sort, but not of the magnitude of the safety factor. I would reveal here what kind of car I drive, but I don't want to give free advertising to a certain Swedish car company.

2. **Climbing a Rock.** Not long ago while visiting a friend's home I happened upon some rock climbing magazines. They contained numerous features on and references to "free climbing" (if I remember the term correctly). This involves rock climbing, often up difficult routes, at great heights, without the safety measure of a belay (i.e., being secured by a rope in case of a fall).

    Now, the climbers who engage in this seemingly treacherous activity tend to be true experts at what they do. Given their expertise and finely honed judgment concerning the limits of their ability, some undoubtedly argue that their great skill takes most of the risk out of it. On the surface this would appear to be true. After all, many of these climbers are able to complete one extremely difficult climb after another without making what could obviously be a fatal mistake. Their reward is presumably a greater gratification upon completing such climbs without external safety measures. I believe however, that their pastime suggests a failure to assess correctly the risk-reward ratio of such climbing. Of course it is the risk that they gauge inaccurately. Arguably, they do assess the risk accurately in the near term; their expertise makes it very small. Each time such a climber undertakes a climb he knows that he will almost surely live to tell about it. The chance of him falling on a given climb may be, say, 1 in 1,000 or even less.

Where they go wrong however, is in assessing the risk over a large number of climbs. Projecting ahead over a large number of these climbs, the risk that at some point a climber will fall becomes ominously greater. Assuming 999-to-1 odds against a fall on a given climb, if we look ahead 1,000 climbs (which might realistically be completed over several years) we find that the chance of a fall — which is highly likely to be fatal — becomes about 63 percent! I wonder if many of these climbers would continue their activity if they analyzed its level of risk in this way.

As if to prove my point, on the day of writing the paragraphs above, I became aware of some anecdotal evidence in support of my conclusions. I was talking about this climbing example with a long time professional poker player who has both a good feel for and an academic understanding of the math involved in risk-reward assessments. This player, known in the poker world as "Gasmask Mike," informed me that as a youth he engaged in similar unprotected climbs, though in a purely "amateur" way with no formal background in rock climbing. Thus, they were certainly much easier climbs, but for an untrained climber no less difficult. Mike guessed that he made about 15 of these climbs. He estimated that on a few occasions, he might have had as much as a 20 percent chance of falling. That was before he had taken up poker and become immersed in the constant risk-reward assessments it requires. He noted, "I only made one of those climbs after I got seriously into poker. After that I just better appreciated the math of it, and realized what an incredible risk it was." (Note that rock climbers can cut their risk of death tremendously simply by using standard equipment and safety procedures.)

3. **Selecting a Medical Provider.** If you are diagnosed with a life threatening illness, such as a serious form of cancer, where should you go for treatment? Most people simply seek treatment in their local area or at the nearest medical center that treats that illness. An alternative is to travel to a major medical center which has established itself as a top center for treatment of that illness. Some people take that option, but some cannot afford the additional expense of such travel, or simply find it too inconvenient. Here the reward is monetary savings and convenience which must be weighed against the potential for an increased risk of death. (There are also emotional elements involved in being away from home and work for extended periods. For the sake of discussion I will specify that I am talking about cases in which this is not a major issue.)

    I contend that when a leading treatment provider has established a track record indicating that treatment there should increase your chance of survival by some statistically significant amount, you should seriously consider travelling there if you are at all able to afford it. Are not the expense and inconvenience worth, say, an eight percent better chance of survival? I suspect that many people receive treatment in their local area simply because there are treatment providers there who are fully trained and qualified to help them. They see that as meeting their requirements. While their local physicians may indeed be so qualified, when you are dealing with your life isn't it wise to look for someone who is not only qualified, but is the best in the field? Weighing risk against reward suggests it is.

Certainly we all risk our lives every day. To minimize our risk of death in the near term would, in fact, drain the vitality from most of our lives. We would never leave our homes. Nevertheless, the examples above suggest that in some areas people may not recognize what is really a disturbingly large increase in their risk of death. Once they do recognize it they can often cut that risk significantly with little loss of the rewards they seek. Moreover, a familiarity with gambling theory and a good feel for risk reward-ratios can help in recognizing such situations. The conclusion? Poker saves lives.

Thoughts on the
Effects of the Poker Literature

Serious poker players sometimes lament the publication of poker books and articles. Writing that offers sound advice, they reason, cannot be good for the games. Certainly good written information will add to the skills of at least some players, but is that all there is to it? Might there be other factors to consider? I believe the question of how the poker literature affects the games is more complex than the simple reasoning typically offered by players who would prefer that high quality poker information be kept secret.

First, what is the basis of the idea that the poker literature makes the games tougher? This belief is simply a common sense conclusion based on a perceived correlation. Players who were playing through the period before and after the publication of most of the major instructional texts (notably the Two Plus Two books) observed that many games gradually became tougher. They attribute this to the books.

This may well be an example of the mistake, well known in science, of equating correlation with causation. A player sees that as "A" occurred (good books grew in number), "B" occurred (games got tougher). He figures A caused B, but he fails to consider either that A and B may have appeared together only coincidentally, or that a third factor, "C," may have been responsible for both A and B.

A Third Factor?

Is there a third factor which may be responsible for both the publication of books and the toughening of games? The publication of many of the better poker books has corresponded with the boom in legalized gambling which began around the late

'80s, and continues today. This boom may in fact have been the "third factor." It clearly caused the publication of books, in the sense that it provided a bigger market for them, but how could it have made the games tougher? The answer is that it brought greater social acceptance of public poker, which led to many more players entering the game from backgrounds previously uncommon for serious poker players. As compared to 20 years ago, a greater proportion of players today are highly educated, often from scientific or other analytical backgrounds. I would venture to say that it has been the gambling boom's bringing in these new types of players, more than books and articles, which has toughened up the games.

It is true, however, that these are also the kinds of players most likely to study books in an effort to learn the game. So I must temper my argument and suggest that it is really the combination of these academically oriented players and the availability of books and articles which has affected the games. Yet even without materials to study, these are the kinds of players who would come to the game with more training in analytical thinking, and who would make more systematic efforts to "solve the puzzle that is poker." Thus I would argue that their presence alone would have made the games tougher.

I would speculate as well that there is another phenomenon, specific to Las Vegas, which has added fuel to the belief that the games have become tougher. This too is a result of the gambling boom. Vegas players noticing the toughening of games may simply be seeing the difference between yesterday's "tourists" and today's. Today's often come from areas where they frequent their own legal public cardrooms. So these people are experienced players, much less "clueless" than the classic tourist who came to Vegas from somewhere with no legal gambling, and sat down to donate for a while in a casino's poker room. It's like having more "locals" come into the game rather than only fun-seeking tourists.

Fear Not the Books

What, then, are the direct effects of books and articles? We can only speculate on this topic. No one has conducted a formal study of the effects on the games or the players. There is only conjecture. It can be intelligent and informed by compelling observations, but cannot identify all the effects with any real confidence. That said, there is no question that some very good players have acquired much of their ability through serious study of the poker literature. Note that I said "serious study." A quick reading of a poker text, no matter how good it is, will not turn a bad player without exceptional intelligence or talent for the game, into a very good one. On the other hand, making a serious project of studying poker from books, combined with much play and independent analysis of the game, just might do it. Add some personal instruction from an expert, and the chance of success rises still further, but only a few players are willing to make this kind of effort. Moreover, some of them, though willing, so lack the temperament or ability to employ the kinds of thinking used in poker that they simply can't break through to real success.

In *Poker, Gaming, & Life,* David Sklansky estimates that of those players who try without studying to become solid winners (making good money in middle limit games, for example), no more than one percent succeed. Of those who do study diligently, he believes about 10 percent succeed.[39] Thus, if we accept Sklansky's numbers — which do seem reasonable — books make a big *relative* difference. Still, they clearly offer nothing close to a guarantee of success.

What about other effects of books and articles? I contend that they have some effects which should be *welcomed* by serious winning players. First, they help create new players, giving beginners information to help them organize their thinking. This

---

[39] Although most certainly do much better than if they hadn't read them.

may give a fighting chance to some who would otherwise lose quickly and give up the game. There are other effects too. They are the effects of which a poker writer is unlikely to feel particularly proud, but which nevertheless benefit the strong winning player worried about his own bottom line.

Consider, for example, a player who's burning up money so fast that he will soon be faced with a choice of either quitting poker, or facing financial ruin. Reading materials may help such a player slow down his losses enough to keep him in the game as a long term modest loser. While this may cost him more in the long run, it should please those whose only interest is their own earn.

Similar is the potential effect on the heavy loser who, because of his losses, plays only sporadically, depending on current cash reserves. The poker literature will sometimes help him become only a modest loser who then plays regularly. This clearly helps games survive and flourish. This, again, must please winning players with any concern about having a game on a regular basis.

Before pointing out another likely effect of written materials, I will make an observation about the prevalence of middle and higher limit games across various poker markets. In small to medium sized markets middle limit games, typically between $10-$20 and $20-$40, are usually the biggest games spread. In the smaller markets there is often no more than one of these games. Often there is nothing even that big. Sometimes such a game is spread only one or two days a week. There simply aren't enough players to support it more regularly. Games at higher limits are often out of the question in these areas, as few if any of the players are prepared to play in them. In the larger markets, middle limit games are much more common, but high limit games (say, above $40-$80) while spread, are relatively few in number. Moreover, they may drop considerably in number on certain days or even disappear from a specific cardroom if not carefully nurtured.

For example, I was at a major cardroom in Los Angeles on three different days during a short period not long before writing this essay. This is a very big cardroom, known for games at limits like $80-$160 and higher. Around the time of my visits, for reasons difficult to pin down, they had experienced a modest decline in their bigger games. Moreover, these games are known to be less consistent on the weekend — another indication of a player base that could stand to be bigger. On a Saturday, I found that the biggest hold 'em game there was $50-$100. On Sunday it was $30-$60. On a subsequent Friday an $80-$160 game started short-handed but quickly broke up. The rest of the day $40-$80 was the biggest hold 'em game. There were always a few names on the lists for bigger games, just not enough on these occasions to get them started. This, while the main floor teamed with countless smaller games. This dearth of games points to the obvious need for more players for games at these higher limits.

In both large and smaller markets, then, there are players for whom there are too few games at the limits they want to play. This is another problem for which poker books and articles may provide a measure of help. What $80-$160 player wouldn't like to always have a few games to choose from every day of the week? Unrealistic? Maybe not, if more players are helped to survive and move up the limits. They need not be world beaters to do this. The poker literature should sometimes help turn a small loser who would never move up from a limit like $10-$20, for instance, into a break even or modestly winning player who might then have the confidence, and maybe the bankroll, to move up to bigger middle limit games or even the higher limits. His entry into these games fills another seat and helps strengthen the player foundation, enabling the games to be spread more consistently, ultimately helping to create new games. Note as well that games at a given limit help support those at neighboring, higher limits.

Many players will play regularly at a higher limit where they might only break even or lose a little. They just want to play at that limit as long as they can survive without getting hurt too badly. Though I would love always to have available games containing only terrible players, I certainly prefer a game with a couple of these mediocre players in it to no game at all.

Thus, books and articles help create games for players wishing to play higher, but whose opportunities are limited. That they do this by improving the skills of some readers is well worth it. Of course, reading will be an important factor in creating a few excellent players, but I am quite sure the mediocre players created in the same way far outnumber them.

So the next time you hear a player complaining that a book or article he is reading is only going to make the games tougher, tell him about the "third factor" and all the games the poker literature creates. If he won't hear it, then simply suggest, "Well, maybe you'd better stop reading. After all, you wouldn't want to make the games tougher — now would you?"

Miscellaneous Topics

Afterthought

No doubt some readers will be displeased with certain of my comments about tournaments, but they represent my genuine concerns about the negative consequences of this aspect of poker. Additionally, at the time of this writing tournaments have received a great deal of attention in the poker media. So a few words to the other side were called for. We need more discussion of the topic, and I hope my essay might encourage that.

I suspect that readers who have long been serious poker players had already considered analyzing various life decisions as risk-reward ratios. But for those a little newer to the game, I hope that my little essay sparked some thoughts about how you approach decisions involving some significant risk. I focused here on the risk of death, but there are lots of other risks involved in life's decisions. Though you need not always take a gambling theory approach to decisions, it can be a remarkably effective tool to which most people are oblivious on anything other than some "intuitive" level.

Perhaps it is not surprising that a poker writer would argue that the poker literature helps poker more than it hurts it. It would be understandable that I would want to defend my decision to write. I could point out that I don't have to write, that the time it takes away from playing poker costs me money. I will say that I would not write about how to play poker if I thought it was going to reduce my hourly rate at the game. As the essay on the topic makes clear, I submit that good poker writing can increase the numbers of middle and higher limit games.

Maybe all of that is dwarfed by another point. The idea that the principles and tactics of skilled poker play can or should remain some sort of inside secret, available only to a few is, in the end, just silly. Not only is this *not* going to happen in this age of accelerating information exchange, with the Internet leading the way, but we simply have no ethical leg to stand on in suggesting that a few people should be privy to information that is purposefully withheld from others.

I predict that, much as with games such as chess, or sports like tennis, nearly all the details of expert poker play will come out in written and other materials. Those who succeed will be those best able to understand and use that information. Knowledge and talent will remain the decisive factors. The only difference might be that new forms of poker may be invented from time to time, providing an extra, albeit short term, edge to those who learn the nuances of those games first. In any case, the players best educated in general poker theory will always have an edge, and will be able to more quickly adapt to and learn the subtleties of new games.

Conclusion

The "poker mind" is remarkably multidimensional. Unless you are a successful "instinct" player who has not studied the game, doing well at poker requires two very different general styles of thinking. You must take the time to think carefully, often slowly through complex concepts as you study poker away from the table. At the table, on the other hand, time constraints demand quick, decisive thinking regardless of situational complexities. A few details may be lost, but you must zero in fast on the most important of innumerable considerations. Beyond these general thinking styles is the need to be able to think in terms of general principles and specific tactical logic, to be attuned to subtleties in opponents' behavior, to be able to see situations from their point of view, and to think and process information in still other ways. Success requires a kind of emotional mastery as well, lest impulse rather than reason influence your decisions. At the same time you must have the intestinal fortitude to be willing to gamble fairly significant money when you know you have the best of it, even when that money figures to be lost more times than not. It is no wonder so few players attain real success.

I have tried with these essays to provide a look at a number of the facets of the mind's work in poker. Of course there is far more to such work than can be contained in one book. Therefore, the best use of this material is as a stimulus for further thought. Let it be one step in a progression as you apply the concepts presented to new situations, or extend them to develop new, related ideas. Be critical of your ideas though, examining them thoroughly and discussing them with others. You do not want to risk significant money on flawed concepts.

If you are striving to move up the limits, perhaps from smaller games up to the middle limits, a number of the ideas outlined should prove helpful. If you are able to think on the levels presented, have learned the specifics of card play, and are relatively uninfluenced by upsetting emotions as you play, you should have little trouble beating almost all games through the middle limits. If you are struggling however, you need to identify the problems and determine how to correct them. Though not necessarily easy, they should not be insurmountable.

If this book has provided interesting reading for you, I am glad. If it has had a positive influence on what goes on for you "inside the poker mind," then I have succeeded.

Index